TAKE ME OUT TO THE
GO-GO

Otakcity Publishing™

TAKE ME OUT TO THE
GO-GO

THE AUTOBIOGRAPHY OF KATO HAMMOND

Otakcity Publishing™

Take Me Out To The Go-Go
The Autobiography of Kato Hammond

ISBN-10: 1508597618
ISBN-13: 978-1508597612

Editor & Consultant — Marlon Green
marlonegreen@gmail.com
www.marlongreen.com

www.tmottgogo.com
www.tmottradio.com

kato@tmottgogo.com

Shout Outs:

Tahira Chloe Mahdi, Denise Young, Renetta Morgan,
Tina Harley-Tobias, Lawand Harley, Brandi Dunnigan,
Samaria Graham, Pam Arrington, Marlon Green,
Preston Blue, Donna Blue, Mark Ward, Nena Brown,
Tyra Berger, Maiah Coles, Rosa "Bud" Jones,
Monica Dorsey, Robert Byrd, Chuck Byrd,
Brian & Diane Ellis, Alex & Charlotte Adderly,
Kenny & Debbie Hammond, Krystina Hammond,
Tamasha Hammond, Dominique Hammond, Iesha Brooks,
Cherrell Brooks, Jeffrey Brooks, Phillice Jackson-Spencer,
Lil Ken Hammond, Kim Lattimore, Tonya Hubbard,
Maria Hammond, Ronald Moten, Eugene Randall,
Jill Morris, Tracy Johnson, The All Around Honies,
Bag of Beats Records, N-Crowd, Crank Brothers,
Go-Go Coalition, The Entire Go-Go Community

Special Dedication to the Memories Of:

Grace Hammond, CB Hammond, Chucky Hammond,
Janie Jackson, Carrie Hammond, June Powell,
Kathleen Grady, Norlishia Jackson, Bernice Mann,
Louie Mann, Robert Jackson, Sr., Rose Jackson,
Phillip Jackson, Yvette Jackson, Tony Jackson, Ronnie
Jackson, Ray Milner, Darnell Queen, Sue Arrington,
Joyce Byrd, Ashley Harley, Joe "Weaze" Carter

Table of Contents

Foreword
by Byron "BJ" Jackson

When I was told Kevin's book was complete, I couldn't wait to see what he was talking about. And after hearing it was about his life, I became even more interested because I knew he had a ton of stories and experiences to share with us. Taking a moment to step back and talk about Kevin is very humbling. We were barely teenagers when I'd play my guitar around him. Most of my cousins and friends watched and enjoyed my keyboard and guitar playing, but Kevin was different. When I played the guitar around him, he focused on what I was doing and always asked questions. It never entered my mind that he went home each time and practiced what he saw me play with the plan of returning to show me how good he was. It was never a competitive thing, it was two teenagers learning, sharing, and getting better.

Kevin's drive was relentless even back then because he did so much with so little. He didn't need a fancy electric guitar to be whole. All he needed was a guitar that he could pluck and do his thing because he'd figure the rest out later. In the meantime, he would practice nonstop, and whenever he returned to my house and played, I could tell that he put in major hours toward his craft. He actually influenced me and made me want to improve through our talking and playing together back then because I didn't have a lot of musician friends to articulate my ideas to and discuss music with. Reminiscing on playing my guitar for him is like smelling the roses because we were only expressing our love of music. That love of music has taken us to places we never imagined.

On the course of playing in groups and doing my thing, I ended up with Rare Essence, and it was interesting to look up and see Kevin right there giving his support. More interesting than his support was hearing about him coming up in the ranks of the music community and making a name for himself on his own accolades. He was in the trenches doing what he loved, and taking the bumps and bruises that came with it. Nothing changed from when we were little because he was still a sponge when it came to music. Knowing that, I always welcomed him to mingle with the members of Rare Essence and to watch our performances from whatever angle his eyes preferred. I knew his mind was taking everything in from the performances. While everyone was partying, he was studying. The next thing I knew, he moved up the ladder and was playing with Little Benny and The Masters. It was cool to hear his name come up musically, it was an honor to have known him while he was coming up, and it was a pleasure to see him on stage. See, I knew what it took to get that far, and I knew what he went through to get to that point. He probably didn't notice because he was on stage performing, but I was watching in admiration every chance I got. Kevin was big time, and he was performing in front of thousands of music lovers.

Suddenly there was someone in my family that was in the Go-Go industry. Being backstage and bumping into Kevin meant I had someone that knew me outside of music. Now I had someone I could talk to about what was going on musically that could understand everything I talked about. Furthermore, I had someone I could talk to without worrying if what I said would be shared with others. It was refreshing to hear what his views on Go-Go were because they came from a genuine place. We'd talk about the music, politics, stories, and philosophies of Go-Go. He never had ulterior motives when he listened and talked. When Kevin has your back, he really has your back. He's also very honest when it comes to his thoughts and opinions. It's a blessing having him in your corner.

I looked up one day and found out he was now known as Kato — he actually earned a nickname from Go-Go, and the name still sticks today. And in addition to playing the lead guitar, he was also on the mic rapping. I know he never imagined that, but anyone that knew of his different skills in high school would have known he was a theatre student in the Duke Ellington School of the Arts. He transitioned into rapping for Proper Utensils as easy as an artist could, and he still had his guitar handy. In addition to that, he was making beats and putting in work in the studio. Kato was driven more than your average artist. Kato the Inner-City Groover was doing all sorts of things in music, and I admired his hustle and his drive.

When I got word that Kato wasn't in a band anymore, I respected his move, and I also respected the fact that he was in the game for a long time. In reality, he wasn't out of the game because he popped up with the TMOTTGoGo Magazine. When I saw the first issue, I was proud, but in a different way than before because this time Kato was in Go-Go from a new angle. And since he is the way he is, I knew he would deliver honest and unbiased content. Soon he was at shows, but instead of a guitar, he had TMOTTGoGo magazines, flyers, and a recorder for interviews.

Wherever Go-Go is, Kato won't be far away. Go-Go runs through his blood. He cares about preserving every aspect of the culture, and he's passionate about it. He's unique in that he was a major Go-Go fan that became a Go-Go artist, and then became a Go-Go historian, while remaining a fan of Go-Go. There's no one else that walked that path. This is the music industry, so he could have easily burned out or turned his back on everything after dealing with disrespectful, dishonest, and crazy people, but he hasn't. He remains a leader in the fight to promote Go-Go to the heights his mind conceives. And after decades in the game, his reputation among artists is still impeccable. Kato is a gift to the Go-Go community and a blessing to those that know him, and I'm proud to be among those he has influenced. If no one has ever told you, I'm telling you now, Kato, I love you, and thanks for everything you've done for Go-Go. We all appreciate it.

Byron "BJ" Jackson

1976

A WALK TO MARYLAND PARK

The sun was setting as I noticed a bunch of people in my neighborhood walking in the same direction. I was only 11-years old, and I had no clue where they were going. George Palmer Highway (Renamed Martin Luther King Highway) was full of folks from all the different neighborhoods in Seat Pleasant, Highland Gardens, Booker T., Glen Willow, Holly Park, Gregory Estates, and the Pleasant Houses, and all of their youth were heading towards Maryland Park across the district line. Since my older brother Kenny was among them, I went on and followed him.

Now although Maryland Park was located across the district line in North East, Washington, DC, I was very familiar with that area because 61st Street is actually where my family was living before my father decided to move out of DC to Seat Pleasant, Maryland. I remember him stating his reason for crossing the district line was because he had gotten into so much trouble growing up in DC that he wanted to try and start a new slate in Maryland. I always thought it was kind of funny how we moved from the DC side to the Maryland side when it was not even a half mile away. Going back and forth to that area was always norm for my sister, my brothers, and me, especially when going to Beulah Baptist Church on Sundays.

On this particular evening, I noticed that the closer we got to Maryland Park, the more I could hear music blaring from the distance. By the time we reached the location, I noticed the large grass field that was normally empty was packed with people standing and crowded together in front of a high stage. On that stage was a live band called The Stratocasters playing a song called "Hey You On The Corner."

IN THE BEGINNING

As far back as I can remember, music has always played a role in my life — not just in the aspect of listening to it, but in the aspect of being part of it.

In my neighborhood, to develop any type of respect, you had to be good in at least one of five things: fighting, sports, music, smooth talking girls, or telling jokes. I learned very early that fighting wasn't necessarily my thing simply because I hated getting punched in the face. When it came to sports, I thought I was okay, but when you're out on the basketball court or football field and you notice that you always get picked close to last, you come to the realization that maybe sports just isn't your thing. I was a pretty funny kid at times, but those times mostly happened during class, and constantly being sent to the office for being the class clown got old quickly. When it came to the girls, I was no Billy Dee Williams, but I was no Woody Allen either. I did okay in that area and had my fair share of girlfriends, but, without a doubt, music was definitely the area where I shined. It was the area where I gained the most respect, and where I was never questioned nor challenged. That was just fine with me because music was the area that I enjoyed spending most of my time anyway.

All the way back to the 4th grade, my friends Tony, Damon, Eugene, and I would write songs and sing them for the kids on the school bus. We called ourselves The Jam Band. Even though we did not have what we considered real instruments, we made decisions as to who would play what instrument when we would be able to get some. I dreamed of that day.

My instrument of choice was the lead guitar. With the exception of the drums, the guitar was the first instrument that really caught my attention. Since we had no instruments, the only thing we had to rely on was our acoustic guitars, which we called "box guitars" or "country guitars." We didn't consider them real instruments, yet, with them, we would record ourselves using little portable tape recorders, and afterwards we would run around the neighborhood asking folks to listen to our tape.

Tony and I spent a lot of our time hanging out at Brigg's Music store, which was located inside of Landover Mall. Every chance we got, we would find a way up there just to hang in Brigg's Music looking at the line of guitars hanging on the racks and predicting which ones we were going to eventually get to take home one day.

Another thing that I would find myself doing every chance that I could was spend time over my cousin Byron Jackson's house. My very first experience with what I considered a real music instrument was through him. Although he was about a year older than me, he was already so advanced and knowledgeable in music that I was always in awe of him. Without a doubt, he is probably the main reason that I wanted to be in music. He played songs on his grey-colored lead guitar, and hearing him play Stevie Wonder's "I Wish" did the trick for me. I would sit in amazement as he ran his fingers across the fret playing the baseline of that song because it actually sounded just like it did on the actual record. I automatically knew that was what I wanted to do, too.

Watching Byron play on his guitar was like a private tutoring session for me that no one but me knew about, not even Byron himself. I would go over to his house and sit there watching him play, then I would go home, grab my acoustic guitar, and try to teach myself all that I just watched him do.

It was a really funny experience for me because every time that I would practice at home and feel myself get a little better, I would then go back over his house to show how much better I had gotten, only to find that he had gotten ten times better than the last time I was over there. Without a doubt, he kept me in awe every time, and he also inspired me even more.

MY FIRST ELECTRIC GUITAR

By no means was my family rich. As a matter fact, I was actually considered one of the poor kids, and I was often teased by some of the kids in the neighborhood for being poor. We were just your average, regular, working-class family. There were six of us: my mother, father, sister and oldest sibling Charlotte, older brother Kenny, little brother Chucky, and me. My father "CB" worked as a truck driver, and my mother Grace, who was a passionate and strong praying woman, worked as an elementary school cafeteria worker, as well as a teacher's aide. With those incomes and 4 children, the idea of asking my father to buy me an electric lead guitar, and him doing it, was not something that I felt was going to happen with ease. In fact, I probably thought it would never happen. Still, that being the only way that I would be able to get one, my thing was to ask him anyway. My plan was to ask my father to buy me a guitar and passionately play on the fact that he was a guitar player who played in a band when he was younger. I figured convincing him from that angle was my only way of even getting him to consider buying one for me.

I asked my father for an electric guitar, and my father came home the next day with a very thick black history book and told me if I were to read the entire book, he would buy the guitar. I opened the book to the back and saw that it had 1,500 pages. Worse than that was the fact that I was not a big fan of reading, especially not a book so intimidating. However, I wanted that guitar. I needed that guitar. I had to have that guitar. Therefore, I had no choice but to read the book, although it was going to be a struggle.

The stories were interesting, but it seemed like I would never get to the end of the book. Eventually, I started scanning through the pages, and every evening when my father would come home from work and ask me to give him details of what I read that day, I basically had to improvise based on the little information I did pick up. Therefore, when I described what I read to him, I basically created my own stories. I was taking a chance that he did not know the full details of any of the stories, and therefore would not realize that I had given him bogus information. It worked because I ended up getting my guitar, and I did so without ever finishing reading that 1,500 page book.

1977-1978

BANDS IN THE NEIGHBORHOOD

Bands playing in different areas throughout the neighborhoods was common. Just about anywhere you went, you could always run into a band playing someplace. Whether it would be at a rec center or playground area, or even in someone's backyard, you could rest assured that the loud music you were hearing from a distance was coming from a live band.

And just about every neighborhood had an official band. For example, in the Fairmont Heights area, there was a band called Black Love. Up in Gregory Estates, there was Aztec. Across the street in the Seat Pleasant Houses was a band that called themselves The Stratocaters. And one of the biggest bands in the area at the time, which was located in Highland Gardens, was a band called Fate's Destiny.

One time while hanging in Belle Haven, we heard what appeared to sound like live music coming from behind one of the buildings. As we dashed around there to see what was going on and who was playing, we noticed three guys with their instruments. One was playing the bass guitar, one was playing the lead guitar, and the other was playing the drums. The amplifiers that they were playing through were plugged into a large extension cord that extended from the 3rd floor of the building they were playing behind. Although there were only three of them, their sound was loud and full. I immediately recognized the song that they were playing as "The Jam" by Graham Central Station.

I was very familiar with the song because it was from one of the dozens of albums that my older brother would play around the house. It was also one of the most popular songs in the area at that time, mainly because of the drum solo that comes near the end of the song. Even though I was used to hearing the song being played on the record, I never heard it before being played live from a band.

Although they sounded like the record, the visual of them playing it made it real. In other words, not only could I hear the lead guitar play his parts in the song, I was able to watch him as he executed through the chords. For some reason, that set my mind on a whole different level. From that point on, I heard the song totally differently than I was hearing it just from the record alone.

NEIGHBORHOOD PEERS

Another thing that was also awesome about having so many bands and kids playing instruments in the neighborhood is that as a younger kid you always had people to look up to — people who you knew directly from your neighborhood. For example, there was this one guy who lived in the building right next to the building I lived named Littlejohn. He was much older than me, and he was playing lead guitar for a band called the Jaguars. Almost every day that I would go outside, I could hear Littlejohn up in his apartment practicing. The guitar would be so loud that it was no question it was him who was in there practicing. Sometimes he would let me come in and sit and watch while he practiced, which was an experience of its own to me.

In Littlejohn's room there really wasn't much furniture other than a bed and a dresser. Everything else was in relation to his music. He had two large guitar amps, a microphone, and a stereo system, and I would sit there watching as he played on his guitar. He practiced as if he was performing live on stage. In other words, he would be standing at the microphone, strumming funky chords as loud as he could on his guitar, consistently going through songs, rudiment scales, solos, and riffs. When he took breaks, he would answer different questions I had regarding his guitar such as the type of strings he used and his execution approach to particular songs such as The Brothers Johnson's "I'll Be Good To You" and Funkadelic's "Cosmic Slop."

Sometimes he would even let me bring my guitar over and teach me different chords and scales to different songs. My favorite of these was no doubt Wild Cherry's "Play That Funky Music." The reason for this was because not only was it such a funky song to strum chords through, but also it was a good selection giving me finger coordination plucking through the individual notes up and down the strings. It was a good practice song that allowed me to stretch my fingers more than I was able to at that time.

Kevin and Dwayne Lee also allowed Tony and me to sit in and watch during their rehearsal sessions. They were brothers who played with The Stratocasters, the same band I saw when I followed my brother to Maryland Park. Although Kevin was much older than we were, his brother Dwayne was just two years older than us, and we got to connect with him in junior high school. Tony and I entered the 7th grade, and Dwayne was in the 9th grade. To us, it was a big deal to be able to connect with Dwayne via school because the Stratocasters was one of the main bands that we got to see often and looked up to, and Dwayne was the keyboard player and also the youngest member.

The major difference between sitting in rehearsal sessions with Littlejohn compared to Kevin and Dwayne was Littlejohn was an individual person, while The Stratocasters held rehearsal sessions in Kevin and Dwayne's basement. The privilege of sitting in sessions of a whole band and not just one person was phenomenal, so we were grateful for the rare occasions they were in a good mood and allowed us to sit inside of the basement while they rehearsed. And when they didn't let us come in, we would be in their backyard standing outside holding our ears to the basement door trying to hear every note. They would play songs such as Earth Wind and Fire's "I Write A Song" and Parliament's "Rumpofsteelskin."

That was actually the beginning of a whole new era for us during that time in junior high school because we were able to connect with even more people from different parts of Seat Pleasant. And the more people we met, the more musicians we met of our age. It was then that we decided to start our own band, but this time it would be a real band. I had my new guitar, Tony had his, and we met a drummer from school named Curtis Brooks, who happened to live in the same development as Kevin and Dwayne.

Every evening after school, Tony and I would grab our guitar cases, head up to Curtis' house, and practice in his backyard: Tony on bass guitar, Curtis on the drums, and I was on the lead guitar. Since we practiced outside, many spectators came into the yard and watched us practice. We were actually performing mini concerts even though we were not concert ready. Before long, other kids who played instruments would come through and join us, and we would have little jam sessions. We learned to play songs like Brick's "Ain't Gonna Hurt Nobody," Slave's "Slide," and the Rolling Stones' "Miss You."

It had actually gotten to a point that our little band, although nowhere near the level of The Stratocasters, was generating small talk among other kids around the neighborhood. Because of this, some of the older kids began to take us a little more seriously. We called ourselves Central Jam, and just like every other "official" band in the neighborhood, we took our trip to Landover Mall to get our band's name printed on t-shirts. Yes, we thought we were really doing something, and, in a sense, we were. This was actually the birth of good things to come for me further down the line musically because the more we played, the more I practiced. The more I practiced, the more I wanted to play and practice. It had gotten to the point where practically every time you saw me, there was a guitar in my hand.

Eventually, The Stratocasters, specifically Kevin and Dwayne, took us under their wing. They coached us through songs, taught us rifts and chords, and even gave us a new name. They called us Baby Strat, and we wore the name like a badge of honor. Therefore, although we were nowhere near the level of the other bands in the area like Stratocasters, Black Love, Fate's Destiny, Aztec, and the Jaguars, we did get the opportunity to play. We performed in people's backyards, behind the buildings of Gregory Estates, at the Seat Pleasant rec center, and even at our junior high school talent show.

BUSTIN' LOOSE

I really wanted to take guitar lessons, but I didn't bother asking my parents. They had four kids to take care of, and they already blessed me with a guitar, so I wasn't going to burden them by asking for more money. Therefore, I began simply trying to teach myself.

The way that I taught myself to play was with records. My older brother always bought records and our bedroom was full of them. Name a group, and most likely my brother had their records lined against the wall on the floor. While both of my brothers would be in the living room somewhere watching football or a TV show, I would be in the bedroom by myself just playing records. When I finally had a guitar of my own, I could strum my guitar and mimic the chords instead of just sitting there enjoying the music. I had the records spinning over and over again while trying to learn how to play the songs. This didn't take any discipline because there was nothing I'd rather be doing. Learning the songs on my guitar was so much fun for me. I didn't realize at the time, but this was called "learning by ear," also known as "the poor man's music lessons."

During this time, two of the hottest songs that were being played on the radio and heavily rotated at the skating rinks were "Aqua Boogie" by Parliament and "Bustin' Loose" by Chuck Brown and The Soul Searchers. Consequently, those ended up being two of the songs that I would sit in my room trying to teach myself.

1979

THE CAPITAL CENTER

The Capital Center was the largest arena in Maryland, and it's where the NBA's Washington Bullets, the NCAA's Georgetown Hoyas, and the Washington Capitals played, and concerts there became major events in our area. It was the only place we got the chance to see big groups such as The Bar-Kays, Confunkshun, Heatwave, Cameo, Lakeside, Brass Construction, Pleasure (70's group), Parliament/Funkadelic, and my all-time favorite Maze featuring Frankie Beverly.

Whenever a show would come to town, we would hustle to try and make the $8 needed to get a ticket. It was like an every-man-for-himself type of thing. First, you needed to get the money to buy a ticket, then you needed to find a way to get to the show.

One of the most popular things that the kids in the area used to do was go to the Crown gas station with arms full of towels to dry off cars as they exited the carwash. The dryer of the carwash was broken, which meant the cars would still be dripping water when they exited. As they pulled out, we would be standing at the end asking if they wanted their cars dried off. The ones who said yes would pull over to the side, and we would dry off all the access water. Each car that we dried off would earn us one dollar. If the person was in a good mood, they would even pay two.

Because a lot of kids from the different neighborhoods in the area would be their trying to get their hustle on as well, it would practically take us an entire day to make just enough money to go to the Capital Center, but once we met our quota it was on, and the night's event was in full motion.

RARE ESSENCE - PG COLLEGE

One Saturday evening as I noticed my older brother and a group of his friends piling into a car, I ran up to them and asked if I could go with them. I had no idea where they were going, but because they were going, I wanted to go. To my surprise, my brother said it was okay, so I got into the car. Having no idea where we were going, I finally noticed that we were entering the parking lot of Prince George's Community College. I had no idea why we were there, nor what was going on there, but I immediately noticed that the parking lot was so full of cars that it was hard finding a place to park.

When we got out of the car we could hear music from a live band, and as we walked towards the field I noticed a large bandstand. It instantly reminded me of the day years earlier when we walked up to Maryland Park and watched bands play. People were everywhere dancing and enjoying themselves as the band on the stage performed.

As I got into the atmosphere and the groove of the music, the band finished their set. That's when I heard people talking about other bands that performed there earlier in the day. I wished I knew about the event because I sure enough would have been there when it began so that I could see every band. It was then announced that there was going to be one final band performing for the evening.

As I stood there watching these guys take the stage, one of the first things I noticed was they were all dressed the same in red sweat suits. Seeing bands dress in uniformity was something that I was used to seeing from the big bands at the Capital Center concerts, but this was not something that I was used to seeing when watching bands in the neighborhoods play. This band also had more members in it than I was used to seeing. Just like the big groups that played at the Capital Center, they had an entire percussion section, an entire horn section, and an entire keyboard section.

Before they began playing, there was a skinny guy that walked up to the microphone at the center of the stage and began talking to the crowd. What he said is something that I still remember to this day, "Today we're going to play some songs that you've heard, and some songs that some of you have never heard before." And then immediately, like a powerful gust of wind, they jumped into action.

They played songs that I recognized such as Kraftwerk's "Trans-Europe Express" and Roberta Flack and Donny Hathaway's "Back Together Again," and just as the guy stated, they also played songs that I had never heard before.

These guys weren't much older than I was, but their playing was more defined and precise than what I was used to. They did all sorts of things with their music that generated spurts of excitement from the crowd. They actually talked directly to the crowd, and the crowd talked back to them; and it had a mesmeric, tribal, ceremonial-type of vibe to it as if the people in the crowd knew exactly what to say and when to say it.

They had gimmicks that had the crowd going crazy. Even though they played songs such as Trans-Europe Express, they played them differently than the original recording, mainly because this version was percussion driven.

Not only did this group have choreographed dance steps, but every song they played had different dance choreography. Everything about their performance had uniformity. They not only played great music, but they put on a show. I was only 14-years old, but I still recognized the difference.

One of the biggest things I noticed about them was, with the exception of the Roberta Flack/Donny Hathaway piece, they never stopped playing, but rather transitioned from one song to the next.

For example, they would play a song, and at the end of it, they would do a strong roll on the percussions, and then drop everything off to nothing but percussion. That made the crowd go crazy. Afterwards, the tall, skinny guy would ask the crowd something like, "Are y'all tired yet?" and the crowd would collectively yell back to him, "Hell no!"

Again, although I had never seen this band, nor heard them play before, there was something about them that immediately drew my attention more than the bands I had seen at the Capital Center. They were different than what I was used to.

There was one particular member of this band that demanded everyone's attention within earshot as soon as he spoke into the microphone. He had the *it* factor, and the crowd responded to his every word and action. He was a short guy with a small frame, but his voice was vociferous and strong, and it received the attention that it commanded.

I started noticing that the tall, skinny guy was referring to the different members in this band by name. For example, when they would go into the percussive interludes, he would yell, "Jungle Boogie!" and as they were in the percussive interlude, the crowd would chant, "Jungle Boogie!" over and over. I found out that was the conga player's name, and everybody shouting for him meant they wanted more of him. The short guy was being referred to by the crowd as Little Benny. The tall, skinny guy doing all the talking was being referred to as Funk.

Although I heard their name mentioned in event promotions on the radio, this was my very first time seeing them. They called themselves Rare Essence. I remember going home that night thinking about nothing but the band I had just seen. At the time, I did not realize how that particular evening affected me, but it changed my perception of the art of performing on stage. Little did I know this was only the beginning of what was to come.

EU - TROUBLE - CLUB LEBARON

Just one week later after seeing Rare Essence for the first time, my brother came home from work and asked if I was interested in going out with him to see another band. He was telling me that a guy he works with plays in the band and they were going to be playing at the Club LeBaron that evening. Still on a high from seeing Rare Essence, I was more than excited to go with him again. Since the Club LeBaron was located in Palmer Park, which was not too far away from where we lived, I figured that it probably wouldn't be a big deal with me being 14-years old, and if it was, it would be easy for him to just quickly drive me back home.

This was going to be my first time ever being inside of a club and that type of atmosphere. With the exception of the Capital Center, the only places I saw bands play were in neighborhoods and rec centers. I knew about Club LeBaron, but I had never been inside of the building. I got to thinking about how I was entertained just a week ago seeing Rare Essence, and I thought to myself how this time I wanted to be able to at least take my tape recorder inside and record the bands. That way, I would be able to listen to them over and over again whenever I wanted to. I grabbed my tape recorder, and my brother and I headed out the door. Just as my brother predicted, we did not have any problems at the door with them asking my age. I don't think they even took notice of it.

There were three bands scheduled on the card to play that night. I can't remember the name of the first band, which was the band my brother's friend was playing in, but they were already on stage playing when we walked in.

The next band to take the stage was a group called Experience Unlimited. Just like the week before, this was a much larger band than I was used to seeing. They were equipped with full percussion and horn sections within their stage setup, and they also did not stop playing in between songs. As they began to play, I hit *Record* on my tape recorder and became so mesmerized by the band that I just stood directly in front of the stage and watched them. People were dancing throughout the club, but my interest wasn't in the dancing. I was all about the music and every nuance within it. I observed the band and took mental notes. Since I had my tape recorder with me, I knew that I would be able to listen and study the music even more when I got back home.

Within this large band was an individual playing the bass guitar that really caught my attention just like Funk of Rare Essence did because he did a lot of talking to the crowd. His name was Sugar Bear, and just like the crowd reacted to Funk a week before, this crowd responded to everything Sugar Bear was saying.

This style of talking to the crowd was brand new to me, and I liked it. It made their performance more personal. I had never seen where bands would talk directly to the crowd in this type of fashion. Usually when we would see a band, they would just play a song, stop, say thank you, and then play another song. The only thing vocally you would hear from them mainly were the lyrics of the songs they were playing.

Everyone highly looked up to Sugar Bear when it came to stage presence and performance. His style and swag dominated any stage that he performed on, and he raised the energy in the venue. His tool was the bass guitar. Sugar Bear wasn't into all the dancing and stage choreography, and he still had a unique way of putting on a hell of a show. The connection he had with his audience was, and still is, top tier.

The difference with Sugar Bear was that, unlike Funk, he played an instrument, the bass guitar, while he talked. Another thing that caught my attention was a bass solo that he had done because powerful bass solos were extremely rare. I constantly listened to people like Larry Graham of Graham Central Station and Louis Johnson of The Brothers Johnson, but Sugar Bear's solo was actually different from theirs. It was the first bass solo that I had ever seen executed in such a pristine fashion. It wasn't funky with thumbing and plucking — it was more towards a style of Rock. He actually played his bass guitar as if he was playing a solo on the lead guitar. It had even gotten to a point in his solo where he grabbed the microphone stand and just scratched up and down on the strings of his bass with it. That definitely looked "Rock" to me. And at the very end of this solo, he fingered into a tune that I was all too familiar with called "The Sailor's Hornpipe." It was a number that I was used to hearing at the very top of the intro of the *Popeye the Sailor Man* theme.

When Experience Unlimited finally exited the stage, there was still one final band left to play. Their name was Trouble (They changed the name to Trouble Funk years later). Now this was a band that I heard of before because my brother bought a record they released called "E-Flat Boogie." Although Trouble's sound was totally different from the other two bands, their set played the exact same style of continuation between songs and they had a man up front who talked to the crowd as well. His name was Big Tony, and he also played the bass guitar.

Although each band was different, there was something about their styles that had my attention like a magnet. Rare Essence was more groovy, Experience Unlimited leaned more towards a heavy Rock sound, and Trouble had a much stronger and powerful Funk sound. These bands shattered the perception I had of how bands could play music. I was conditioned to play songs and then stop after each one like the bands I saw in the local neighborhoods. However, my paradigm shifted. From that moment on, whatever band I was playing with, I wanted us to play that exact same style of continuing playing without stopping for breaks between songs.

One of the biggest reasons I wanted to change styles was because of the feedback that they were receiving from the crowd. It was more energetic, and the crowd was more involved than what I had been used to seeing. The success of it consisted of 50% band performance and 50% audience participation. It was a new genre of music that was given the name Go-Go.

THE EMERGING OF GO-GO

The very first thing that I wanted to do when I got back around the neighborhood was to connect with the fellas and talk to them about the style that I had seen. I wanted us to learn to play that same style, but it wasn't easy for me because it was very hard to put into words and describe exactly what I was trying to say. Actually, to a few of them, it didn't really make any sense for a band to play and never stop in between their songs. Some of the bands, such as Black Love, were adapting this style into their sets. And other bands, such as The Stratocaters were choosing not to. Nevertheless, I still wanted to learn that style.

I would play the tapes that I had of Experience Unlimited and Trouble all the time, over and over again. I studied them while wishing that I also had my tape recorder when we went to see Rare Essence because the tapes gave me the ability to visually recollect exactly what the band did. It made it easier for me to remember the styles in which they transitioned from one song to the next. I played those tapes while learning the songs they played on my guitar, or rather I was teaching myself the songs they played.

Not too long after this, the band called Experience Unlimited put out a record called "Rock Ya Butt." And as a student of Go-Go music, of course, I immediately ran out to get it as soon as I heard about it.

In truth, this whole new style was actually created by the band Chuck Brown and The Soul Searchers, the same band who had just released that hit record called "Bustin' Loose." My being so young at the time, I had no idea that they were also a local band from the area. In fact, one of the regular spots where they played was a small club just up the road from me called Ebony Inn. Since I was just a kid, they were not on my radar. But my father and his friends would always go to see them play.

DUKE ELLINGTON SCHOOL OF THE ARTS

The age of 14 was also the year of my wake-up call. Along with new discoveries came new experiences, mistakes, and lessons learned. This was my 9th grade year in junior high school, and I was slowly, but surely, coming of age.

While at a party, I met this girl who I began dating pretty seriously. She lived in South East, DC, which was a pretty far distance for a young man that was too young to drive, so many times I found myself traveling out there on the bus to kick it with her at her house. One of the biggest things that I really loved about this girl was that she could sing her ass off. During the times when we would be cuddled up at her house, she would always sing for me. Man, I would be in such a zone by her tone. Our love for music was the biggest thing that we had in common. She would sing, and I would play my guitar. Our favorite was "Cruisin" by Smokey Robinson.

During that time, we were both in our last year of junior high school and just about ready to start attending high school. Because of our passion for music, she began telling me that she would be attending a certain arts high school in DC that specialized in music. The school was called Duke Ellington School of the Arts, and in order to be able to attend, you had to first of all live in DC. Second, you had to audition to get in. She already auditioned and was accepted, and she thought it would be a good idea if I auditioned as well so that we would be able to attend high school together.

Although I felt I should have had no problem in handling the auditioning part, the only problem that I faced was that my family no longer lived in DC. Later, I found out that you could attend the school living in Maryland, but you had to pay a tuition. That was something that, of course, my family could not afford to do, but still I wanted to go badly; not necessarily just because my girlfriend would be there, but merely because I felt that place and atmosphere was where I needed to be artistically. Just the thought of being able to attend a school where the majority of what I did was learn and play music all day long excited me to no end. So with my grandmother's permission to use her South East, DC address, I decided to go audition.

The day of the auditions was a very big moment for me. Although I had no idea exactly what the audition would consist of me doing, I was more than ready to find out. I knew that I wasn't a great guitar player yet, but I looked at this as my opportunity to finally get extensive training in the proper areas.

Duke Ellington was located in the Georgetown area of North West, and in order to get there from Seat Pleasant, I had to take two different buses. By the time I got there, one of the biggest things that I noticed about the school was that it looked nothing like a school at all. The old, white, rundown building that towered at the top of a grassy hill had the appearance of some sort of colonial-style library. I remember thinking to myself, *This is the big, bad school of performing arts that I've been hearing so much about?*

The first thing I thought when I got off the bus was that maybe I was in the wrong place. The only thing that stopped me from turning around and going back home was that there were teenage kids everywhere! That actually excited me more, while at the same time made me a tad bit nervous. This was brand new territory to me. The entire atmosphere was totally different from what I was used to. Inside the building was just like outside on the front lawn; kids were everywhere!

As I sat in the large music room with the other kids waiting for my turn to be called into the auditioning room, something very uncomfortable dawned on me. It appeared to me that the one thing every kid in that room and I did not have in common was that they all knew how to read music and I didn't. I inquired from a few others and found out another stipulation that you had to have in order to be accepted was you had to already know how to read music.

That revelation floored me because learning how to read music was one of my main reasons for wanting to attend the school. With that newfound discovery, I quietly gathered my things and walked out.

As I began to leave the building, I noticed another auditioning session happening at the other end of the building. This one was for people who wanted to attend the school majoring in Theater. As far as I knew, there wasn't a need to know how to read music in acting. And somehow, some way, I had to get into this school. So instead of leaving the school altogether, I thought to myself, *Why not?* and proceeded to that area to try my luck at acting and finding out for sure how bad I really wanted to be in that school.

It was true that I didn't need to read music in order to be accepted in the theater department, but what was needed was an audition with some type of already prepared monologue. I explained to Donal Leace, who was director of the theater department at the time, that I did not know I needed to have a prepared monologue. I then asked him if I could come back tomorrow and try again. He said that I could.

That night, I spent hours learning the lines and practicing in the bathroom mirror a scene from the movie *Brian's Song*. By the time the morning came, I was confident in myself that I would do great.

Back at the school and ready to audition, Mr. Leace remembered me from the day before. He called me to come forward and audition, and by the time I was done with my monologue, I was in. My audition was successful and I had now been accepted to go to the Duke Ellington School of the Arts.

Although I personally felt I did a great job on my audition, the real reason that I got in was that Mr. Leace was impressed I came back. Either way was fine with me. All that mattered to me was that coming in the fall, I would officially be a student at the Duke Ellington School of the Arts.

Or would I?

THE WAKE-UP CALL

Just as swift as I got accepted at Duke Ellington, it was equally as swift putting myself in a position that could end with my not being able to go there after all. This period marked the point of my first wake-up call.

As I mentioned earlier, 14 began my coming of age years, but it also began a time of getting in trouble. The 9th grade for me presented a string of temptations. I stayed in trouble a lot for cutting school. On many occasions, a group of guys and I would, instead of going to our own school, take the day off and do things we considered more fun and adventurous. Other times, I would take off alone and a ride to Hart Junior High School located in South East, DC to visit my girlfriend.

On one particular occasion, a buddy and I decided that instead of going to school, we would head up to Landover Mall and do some shopping. The only problem with that was neither of us had any shopping money. That was one of quite a few situations that ended up with me getting arrested for shoplifting, and my father getting called to come pick me up.

Needless to say, those type of things resulted in my facing the possibility of repeating the 9th grade or going to summer school. I picked summer school. By that time, I had already been accepted at Duke Ellington for the fall, and having to repeat the 9th would mean that I wouldn't be able to attend.

One day as I was coming home from summer school, a group of older guys that I knew called for me to come join them as they headed towards the back area of the complex. By the time I got over to where they were, they began climbing up the side of a building and breaking into an apartment, so I climbed and entered it with them. I personally didn't take anything from the apartment, but that still didn't change the fact that I went in there.

Later, one of the older guys was spotted by the police walking up the road carrying a television set. When they stopped him and discovered that the television set had, indeed, been stolen, that was when he snitched on everyone else including me.

By this time, my father had grown tired of me and was just about ready to send me to Boys Village, which was a school for delinquent children. The only reason that he didn't was because my mom refused to let him, but that wouldn't be enough to stop me from going there because, as a result of the incident, I was given a date for a hearing for the courts to decide if they were going to send me there anyway. The only thing that stopped them from doing so was them finding out I had been accepted to the Duke Ellington School of the Arts. Giving me a second chance, they ended up just putting me on probation instead. Therefore, that following fall, I was, indeed, an active student at the Duke Ellington School of the Arts.

1980

FINALLY AT DUKE

From the very first moment I arrived at Duke, it was a whole new world to me. Everything was different from what I had been used to.

This was also my very first experience in being up close and personal with kids who were playing in neighborhood Go-Go bands. Even though they were fellow students at Duke studying courses in Jazz, Blues, and Classical, outside of the school, they were also members of different neighborhood bands throughout the city. People like Donnell Floyd and Harold Little, who were horn players with Chance Band, Lil Mike, who played trumpet with Petworth, Hard Rock, who was playing guitar with The Peacemakers, and many students who played in other bands such as Ovation, Mass Extinction, Ayre Rayde, and others attended. Therefore, along with the taste of learning my craft in the theatre department, my experience, growth, and knowledge of the Go-Go scene rapidly grew stronger there as well. It was common during lunch period for kids to gather in a particular area and listen and dance to whatever the hottest, newly-released PA tape ("PA" refers to the Public Address system which music was recorded from).

At one point, there was even a group of kids who formed a Go-Go band in school, and during a lunch period they would practice in the boys' locker room area that hovered over the gym. This would create an event every day where kids would gather in the gym during that lunch period just to listen to them practice. In a sense, we were having our own Go-Go right there in the school every day. If my memory serves me correctly, I believe they called themselves the Locker Room Band based on that experience. Although they really didn't last that long together as a band, never once moving their show from the locker room practices to the actual Go-Go stage at a club, they really sounded tight and used to have a straight party going on during those practice/event sessions. A few of the members of the Locker Room band were already active members in the neighborhood Go-Go bands. Undoubtedly, the taste of that experience was priceless, and the impact it had on me artistically further fueled my love and interest for Go-Go.

Of course, not every student was into Go-Go music nor its scene like I was. In fact, many students despised and made fun of it. They would refer to it as "jungle music," and refer to those who appreciated it as "block boys." Basically, it was just another way of calling us neighborhood ghetto kids. I always found that kind of funny because they were essentially from the same neighborhoods as we were. They just weren't into the Go-Go music, and that separated us in a major way.

THE TNT POPPERS

Another growing phenomenon that was gaining momentum with the youth during this time was a popular street dance that we called "The Pop." It was also referred to as The Electric Boogaloo and Pop Locking. This was a dance that was essentially made popular by folks such as Shabadoo and Jeffery Daniels, and groups such as The Lockers. Although this wasn't actually what was called Break Dancing, it was kin to it and had the same type of street rep. Therefore, along with the areas of kids that would engage themselves in Go-Go music activities during lunch periods, there were also areas where kids would engage themselves in Popping activities by blasting their boombox with songs from groups like Cameo, The Sugar Hill Gang, Dazz Band, and Grandmaster Flash & The Furious Five. They would gather in crowds and have Pop Locking battles.

Around this time, I had become really tight with a group of guys there, and two of them were active participants in the Pop Locking battles. Eventually they formed a dance group and called themselves the TNT Poppers. I was not good at doing this type of dance, but because they had become really close friends of mine, I was able to hang around and attend different performing events with them. One of the biggest events that they took part of was a competition that DC held called the Metro Talent Search. This was a large-scale event that consisted of levels and different rounds within different categories of entertainment, i.e., singing, dancing, and musicianship. In other words, if you would win in one round, you would advance to the higher level of the next round, and if lucky enough, you'd make it to the final round, which took place on the big stage at DAR Constitution Hall, the major concert venue of Washington, DC.

The TNT Poppers were, of course, in the category of dance groups, and they made it to the final round. I was there with them for the entire ride. In fact, I would actually be at home at night doing my homework of practicing and learning the dance myself so that I could also be a member on stage with them. Although I eventually became an active member on the stage with them, I was not able to begin performing publicly with them during the rounds of the Metro Talent Search because they already started and were in the middle of the level rounds.

The TNT Poppers did not win the Metro Talent Search competition, but this event sparked a whole lot of open doors for the group. The members were George Dick, Rodney Little, brothers Chuck & Robert Byrd, Mike Scott, and me, the new member. Performing under the same type of pseudonym as groups such as Parliament/Funkadelic, we all wore costumes and had stage names to match our individual personalities. George was Dr. Popinstein, Rodney was Mr. Fantastic, Chuck was Sir Zapp, Robert was Robonic Locker, Mike was Sir Pop-A-Lad, and I was Little Caesar. We began doing shows, cabarets and events across the city. This also included a few Go-Go events as well. After doing a couple of community events with the Go-Go band Mass Extinction, they began asking us if we were interested in performing at some of their shows.

This is how it worked; they would play a set, and then during their break they would introduce us, and we would come out doing our dance routine. We were a novelty act that added towards the experience of a Mass Extinction show. It was something new that they were trying to incorporate in their events fulltime because it wasn't just us who they would invite to perform, but also other performers around the city. Hence, giving the nuance of knowing that attending a Mass Extinction show entailed more than just the band themselves, but a whole entertainment extravaganza experience. Another act that they had perform during the break was a group of little kids who also played Go-Go music, but they played on buckets, toy keyboards, and toy horns. Like us, they would also perform for about five to ten minutes wowing the crowd until Mass Extinction returned to the stage. These little kids called themselves The Junkyard Band, and eventually grew up to be one of the most popular and influential bands in the history of Go-Go.

SYEP / SHOWMOBILE

One of the biggest things that we as the TNT Poppers had gotten involved with was the Showmobile. Mayor Marion Barry had just initiated a program in DC called the Summer Youth Employment Program (SYEP). This was a program that allowed thousands of teens between the ages of 14 and 21 to enroll in and obtain summer jobs in the DC area. During a time where a lack of jobs drove up crime rates, squalor, and drug use, Mayor Barry's initiative helped spur and encourage us towards early hands-on training and experience, while getting paid for it at the same time. The jobs ranged in different areas from office work to industrial, from retail and hospitality to entertainment. Our job fell under the entertainment category. Individually enrolling in the SYEP and collective as a group, we were hired to work for the DC Department of Recreation, which was directed by Raymond Gray, who was a man that started as our boss and ended up being more of a mentor to us.

The Showmobile, a large tractor trailer that converted into a make-shift stage, was an arm of the Department of Recreation that we worked under. It served as an entertainment gala that would take place in the parks and neighborhoods throughout the city. There would be several of them going on at the same time, all showcasing a variety of live entertainment that included dance groups and live music such as Jazz, R&B and Go-Go bands. This served as a super plus for me because, even though at the time I was working within a dance group, my heart still was with live bands. Being on the card with and constantly around all of these different live bands allowed me to actually latch onto, learn, and absorb essential knowledge and experience from them. Sometimes I was even granted the opportunity to sit in on sessions with my guitar.

Every day we would report to Mr. Gray's office, located on Park Road, and pick up our schedule detailing where we would be performing and which acts would be performing on the same show.

Then we would head over to that location and perform like we were being paid to. The awesome thing about this was not only would the schedule give information about the Showmobile and location where we would be performing, it would also have a schedule of all the different Showmobile locations. This gave us the information we needed should we decide to go and check out another show once our performance was over. For example, we would be on a particular show with other acts such as The Bren-Carr Dancers, Hot Profit Band, and Mass Extinction performing at Malcolm X Park, while, at the same time, other acts such as Rare Essence or Petworth band would be performing at locations such as River Terrace, Rock Creek Park, or Oxon Run. Since I was a Rare Essence head, I would finish my performance at the Showmobile location assigned to us, then jump on the metro bus and head over to another location to watch Rare Essence perform. It basically went that way for me the entire summer.

BREN-CARR DANCERS

One of the connects we made while working on the Showmobile was with a dance company called The Bren-Carr Dancers. These were a group of girls our ages whose choreographed dance performances ranged from Ballet and African, to Jazz and Tap. Since we were a group whose only style of dance was The Pop, which was a style they did not perform, they took a liking to us and began inviting us to perform on other shows with them outside of the Showmobile. Eventually, not only did they invite us to perform on stages with them, they also invited us to perform within their routines. We would go to their rehearsals, which were located at the Eastern Branch Boys and Girls Club in South East, and practice learning Jazz, African, and Tap dancing.

Under the direction of Mrs. Brenda Jordan, The Bren-Carr dancers were known across the city as a dance company to be reckoned with. In fact, not only did they perform, but they also choreographed routines for other stage acts. I discovered that while attending their rehearsal sessions. And one of the biggest acts in city they choreographed steps for was Rare Essence. This was of great interest to me because one of the things that always fascinated me about Rare Essence was the fact they had choreographed steps for every song that they played. This was a technique that other bands who looked up to Rare Essence incorporated in their stage shows as well. In fact, not only did they incorporate this type of presentation in their shows, but they executed the same exact steps. One of the most popular of them all, which many bands still do to this day, is a routine where the entire band, in unison, swing their bodies back and forth from the left to the right, and take a step, while subtly kicking into the air at each swing. The choreography of the bands were amazing, and The Bren-Carr dancers were the main source that taught it.

1981

ACADEMICS

With all the different activities that I had become involved with, it turned out I was not keeping up to par with my academics at Duke Ellington. This is something that if not paid the proper attention to, you could easily fall victim to failing, and I became one of the victims. It was actually very easy to fall into that realm at Duke because what they didn't do was babysit and monitor you the way the regular schools did. If you missed classes and didn't stay up on your assignments, they wouldn't hound you about it. Much like college is, you basically found out your status when your grades came out. Apparently my mental had not yet reached that level of maturity at the time. Therefore, I didn't give much attention to my academic classes at Duke, but I gave plenty attention to the Arts classes that took place in the evenings. In fact, there were times when I didn't even show up for my academic classes. I only took the Arts classes seriously, and unfortunately, you must stay on top of both.

Bottom line, I was screwing up big time, and my not going to my academic classes caught up with me. By the end of the school year, I was informed that I failed and was therefore going to have to repeat the 10th grade. The funny thing about it though, was they let me repeat it there at Duke. It wasn't until my second year there that they finally decided enough was enough and I just wasn't going to get it. They ultimately kicked me out, and I was going to have to go back to the school that kids in my neighborhood had to go to. However, I was far too much into the whole Duke scene at that point to even imagine going back to public school. At the end of the year, I came up with a plan to get back into Duke — I would get my act together, practice a new monologue, and audition again in an attempt to get back into the school.

Just like before, my audition had to consist of a monologue play. I chose to do a piece from the musical *Purlie*. When I entered the room to do my audition, among the judges was Mr. Leace, the theater director who kicked me out. Before I could utter a word of my monologue he interrupted me.

"There is not a single person in this room who does not know that you have talent," he said, "but you brought yourself down, and almost took a few with you. Why did you come back?"

I had no clue what or who he was referring to when he said that I almost took a few down with me. I simply humbled myself and replied, "Because I think I got myself together."

I went on from that point and did my audition piece from *Purlie*. No one in the room uttered a word about my performance, but they were all smiling, and that had given me the impression that they really liked it. At that point, I was confident that I was going to be accepted back into the school.

The next morning, there was a big write-up in the Washington Post newspaper about the auditions held at Duke Ellington the previous day. Among the different stories written about in this article was the audition piece that I did. Seeing this article about me served as my confirmation that I was going to be accepted into Duke Ellington. After all, why would there be a write-up about me in the newspaper if I was not going to be allowed back in. This article even mentioned exactly what Mr. Leace said to me and what my response was to him.

Not long after reading the article, my mother came and told me that Mr. Leace called her and said that I did not make the audition to be accepted back into the school. His reason for not accepting me, as he told my mother, was because of my answer to the question he had asked me. He stated that instead of saying, "I got myself together," I said, "I *think* I got myself together." Because I used the word "think," he didn't believe I was really sure about it. Of course, to me that was petty as hell. I was just a kid. School me. Don't throw trick questions at me and then punish me because I didn't answer the way that you thought I should have. Needless to say, I was heartbroken, but what could I do? His decision had been made. What was done, was done.

CUE

During my time at Duke Ellington, I was fortunate enough to have been able to do more than just Duke. While being there, I found out that a few theater department friends of mine were also members of a theater company for kids outside of school. The company was called CUE, which stood for Children's Urban Arts Ensemble. They told me the company was currently holding auditions for more kids to join, and I also found out they were doing plays and musicals around the city. That really piqued my interest, so I decided that I was going to take my chances and audition for this children's theater group.

They informed me that in the audition, I would have to do a monologue from any play, as well as choose a song to sing. I decided to use the same monologue I auditioned to get into Duke Ellington since it proved to be a successful for me once before. This was a monologue taken from a movie called *Brian's Song* — a scene where Gayle Sayers receives the *George Hollis Award* and in his speech he dedicated the award to Brian Piccolo. Also during this time, I had become very fond of an album my sister had of the Broadway musical *The Wiz*. On the album there was one particular song that was my favorite called "I Was Born On The Day Before Yesterday." A scene and a song from The Wiz were the two pieces that I decided to audition for CUE with. Ultimately those two pieces got me in, and from that point on, I had become a new member of the Children's Urban Arts Ensemble.

Every Friday after school we would rehearse at the Logan Center, which is located right around the corner from Union Station in North East, DC. On Saturdays, we would spend the entire day rehearsing at a secluded rec center that would be closed for the day and available only to us for rehearsal. At the time we were preparing for a musical production entitled *CUE On Broadway*. This was going to be a production where we were going to be performing familiar scenes from a variety of different Broadway shows to include *The Wiz, Annie, A Raisin in the Sun, Purlie*, and *Don't Bother Me, I Can't Cope*.

Our rehearsal sessions were very strenuous and very strict. The company was founded and run by a woman named Michelle Fonville Johnson. The ensemble had very talented kids from all across the city. Our ages ranged from 10 to 18. I was 16 at the time, and, without a doubt, I was having a great time being fully immersed into the arts. I was overwhelmingly influenced by the experience I received while with CUE, and I was highly inspired by Mrs. Johnson and the work that she and the rest of her staff put into molding us for that experience so much that it was the best I had in my life. When it came to working through the choreography of the different production pieces that we performed, she brought in top-notch choreographers such as LaVerne Reed, and musical directors such as Steve Lawrence.

The experience that I gained and learned from CUE was unmatched by any other stage experience that I encountered to that point, and that includes Duke Ellington and Street Theatre. At the age of 16, I was performing on stages in venues everywhere. For example, in the different productions that we performed scenes from, I got to play characters such as Walter Lee Younger in *A Raisin in the Sun*, and Getlow in *Purlie*. As a company, we performed in different places throughout the city including The Gallaudet Auditorium and The Kennedy Center. We even went on a trip to New York to see a new hit Broadway musical called *Dream Girls*, and afterwards we got to meet the cast of the play later that night. Meeting Sheryl Lee Ralph, Clevant Dereks, and Loretta Devine was wonderful. While on that same New York trip, we even got to perform some of our musical production in front of The Lincoln Center. Even though I had been torn apart by being kicked out of Duke Ellington, thanks to CUE, I was still able to be very active in the theatrical aspect of entertainment.

1982

BOWIE HIGH SCHOOL

Getting kicked out of Duke Ellington meant that I had to return to the school that kids in my neighborhood had to go to, and since I was now in high school, that school turned out to be Bowie. I had been away from the kids in my neighborhood so long while attending Duke that I was somewhat out of touch to the daily ins and outs of what had been going on in the neighborhood. My experience with the situations I encountered and had been doing while attending Duke actually gave me a different outlook, thus my point of view was a bit different from the rest of the kids in the neighborhood. I felt a bit out of touch. The same kids who I had known through elementary and junior high school years had gotten older and more mature just like I had, so it actually took me a little time to familiarize myself with them again and get readjusted to what I considered being back to the norm.

However, one aspect about being at Bowie that I found myself very comfortable in due to the past couple years was Drama class. I didn't need even a minute to adjust myself because I was acting on a high level. It was actually kind of funny the way the students and the teacher in that class treated me because since they knew I had come from Duke Ellington, they treated me as if I were elite in theater. That was when I realized just how much prestige and weight the name Duke Ellington School of the Arts carried.

Even though they looked at me as somewhat superior, and treated me differently in a good way because of where I came from, this was still a predominantly white school, and my being black meant that I was only able to play tiny roles in any of their productions. I couldn't play anyone's husband, father, boyfriend, son, or cousin.

For example, in a production they put on called *You Can't Take It With You*, I was cast in the play as the door-to-door salesman, which was a small part. Since the cast was pretty much all white, and the story was about a family, I wasn't placed in any of the roles despite my acting ability since I didn't look like I could be related to anyone in the rest of the cast.

Another example was when the Bowie drama class participated in the Shakespeare Festival. This was an event that took place every year at the Folger's Theatre, where high schools from all across the metropolitan area gathered in competition with each other performing scenes from Shakespeare plays. We were there to perform a scene from *Romeo and Juliet.*

One of the schools that we had to go up against just so happened to have been Duke Ellington, and in that situation I found myself actually competing with students that I was friends with while I was at Duke. Even more interesting, when Mr. Leace, the director of the theater department at Duke found out that I was one of the students at a school that was in direct competition with him, he took notice and even became a tad bit concerned — that was until he realized the part that I would be playing was so small that I didn't even have any lines. There were only two black people in our production of *Romeo and Juliet*, a black girl in my class and me, whereas my friends from Duke Ellington were doing a scene from Shakespeare's *Othello.* Of course, since Duke was a predominantly black school, their production had a predominantly black cast. Needless to say, they not only wiped us out, they wiped out every school in the competition without even working up a sweat. In truth, I was really happy for them, not because they were from Duke Ellington, but because they were my friends, so in a funny kind of way it felt like I had won, too.

There was one exception at Bowie that I did get to take advantage of, and that was an event that Bowie did every year called the One-Act Play Festival.

As a child, I had known about this festival because my older brother was involved with it when he was attending Bowie. His participation in it back then was only to get a credit toward graduation because he would have gotten a failing grade had he not. As a child, I remember going to see him in this festival and being so intrigued and obsessed about what was going on around me. Now that I was a student at Bowie, I was actually looking forward to participating in it.

The way the One-Act Play Festival worked was all the students in the drama class had to gather in small groups, and each group would pick a one-act play to perform, practice for a week, and then perform in front of a live audience the night of the event. At the end of the event, there would immediately be an awards ceremony, and the awards were given based on the judge's votes. The categories were Best One-Act Play, Best Costume Designs, Best Actor, and Best Actress.

In our class, the seniors were directors. They would decide the one-act play that they wanted to direct, and then they would choose the cast members from the rest of the students in the class. I was chosen by a white girl, who actually told me that she chose me because I was black, and she wanted to challenge herself to see if she could direct me in a type of production that was totally different from the types of roles that I had been playing at the school thus far. The play was a two-character play entitled *A Wisp in the Wind*. The only other character beside me was played by another white girl.

The story was a comedy about two strangers who find themselves deeply engaged in the strangest but funniest conversation while sitting at the bus stop. We put on a great performance, and I was confident that I put my all into the character I played. While sitting in the audience with my mom at the end of the night, the host said, "And the winner for *Best Actor* is a person who we all feel has a tremendous amount of talent…Kevin Hammond!" I won Best Actor for the entire event. Needless to say, it was what I always dreamed of achieving when I was little.

THE CREATIVE PROCESS OF FORMATTING A SONG

Although I was really deep into theatre, music was my first love, and it was no secret how much of a Rare Essence fan I was. Yes, I had become a big fan of Go-Go in general, but even more, I had become a fiend of Rare Essence. Every chance I got, I would go see them play. I would make it my business to get a copy of every PA tape that hit the streets. I even walked around high school with a Rare Essence notebook that I designed. On the cover, I drew the large RE logo inside of a circle with wings extending from the "R." On the inside cover, I sealed a picture of the band from a Washington Post newspaper article. And, on the back cover, I drew pictures illustrating some of their songs such as "Get On The Wagon," "Take a Little Ride Through The City," "Roll Call," "One On One," and "Take Me Out To The Go-Go."

I was also always in debates with some of the kids at school about who was better between Rare Essence, Ayre Rayde, Experience Unlimited, and Trouble Funk.

When it came to going to see them at places such as the Howard Theatre, instead of being on the dance floor partying with the rest of the people, I would be on the balcony leaning on the rail and just watching and observing them play. Or in other places, such as the Maverick Room and the Panorama Room, I would stand to the left or right side of the stage, again just watching and observing them play.

I would take mental notes of the way they transitioned from song to song. I would watch as they executed different choreography steps for each song they transitioned to. I picked up on how they would vamp into the songs that they were playing. It took lots of time and close attention to catch the cues they used to communicate to each other what direction to take the songs because they were done in several ways including vocally incorporating the cues into songs or doing them with subtle hand signals. I would watch how they took pieces of known covered songs, revamp them, and then convert them into something that would later become theirs. This was something I termed "The creative process of formatting a song into Go-Go."

For example, there was a particular song by The Chi-lites they used to play called "Bottoms Up." This was a selection that really caught the crowd's attention, mainly because of a chant that went:

"There's a party over here. There's a party over there.
Before you know it, there's a party everywhere.
Jam, jam, jamming on the left.
Jam, jam, jamming on the right.
But any way you move when you move that bottom,
you know it's going to be all right.
So moooove that bottom. Shoo be do wop that bottom."

In the original Chi-lites version of this song, there is a measure of a flute line that plays over and over. The flute line was so minute in the song that many people actually didn't take notice of it, and it only played during the very end of the song. Well, Rare Essence took this little flute line, designated it to the horn section, added strong staccato punches to it, and, in turn, made it into one of the dominant aspects of the song. Now that it was dominant, they placed it at the top and used it as a powerful intro into the song. They then included their own hook, lyrics, and a new bass line. Of course, there were more parts added, removed, and changed, but you get the gist of where I'm going. Before you even realized that it was happening, it happened. The selection now sounded like a totally different song because it was, indeed, a totally different song. No longer playing The Chi-Lite's "Bottoms Up," but instead they were now playing their brand new song called "Shoo Be Do Wop," which, of course, was birthed from "Bottom's Up."

My experiences in the theatre are the roots of what encouraged me to pay attention to those type of things when watching bands play. I had become more aware at paying closer attention to not just the music being played, but also the presentation in the areas which music was being delivered.

I also paid attention to how band members were organized into sections on stage. First, there is the frontline. They are the people who are closest to the audience and communicate with them. They are the faces and voices of the band. They are also the first thing that your average audience pays attention to.

Next is the middle section, located in the middle of the stage. These are most likely the rhythm section, consisting of bass and lead guitar players, horn players, and keyboard players. This section is very mobile. They can step back to communicate with the backline, as well as step forward to communicate with the frontline. Sometimes they even participate with the frontline.

Then there's the backline, which consists of the driving force of the band: the drums, congas, and other percussion instruments.

1983-1984

YOUNG PLAYWRIGHTS FESTIVAL

Needless to say, I was a very busy teenager. Although my mom and dad did not quite know nor understand what I was doing, they did know that it was something positive, so in their own way and to the best of their ability, they always supported. They never really asked me questions about it, but they never really stopped me either. What they did understand was I was definitely doing something right despite all the disappointments and stumbling blocks I had run into up to that moment; especially with just a couple of years prior they were trying to decide if I should go to Boy's Village or not. There was no question that I kept myself busy doing positive activities, and that seemed to be good enough for them.

There was, indeed, a whole lot going on. I was still involved in CUE, I started back practicing in jam sessions with some of the bands in the area, and I was involved with the drama class at Bowie. That was not enough evidently because I was just about to become involved with a whole new endeavor that would broaden my focus and view.

While in drama class one day, the same white girl who I worked with on the one-act play had come up to me and asked if I was going to submit something to the Young Playwrights Festival that was held in New York every year. I had no clue what she was talking about, so she explained to me that the festival is a playwriting competition for teens held annually. If you wrote and submitted a play into that competition, you could have the chance of having that play produced in New York City. At minimum, if you weren't chosen, your play would at least get critiqued by them. As she gave me a copy of the information and submission form, my interest piqued once again. I already started writing a play for no real specific reason, but since this Young Playwright competition was taking place, I found myself wanting to hurry up and finish so that I could enter the competition. The only problem was there was only one week left before the deadline for submissions.

With the help of my sister and my godmother, both allowing me and teaching me to use their typewriters, I eventually finished my play and sent it off to the competition.

About four months later, I received a letter and then a call from New York. Out of 1,160 plays submitted, the Young Playwrights Competition broke it down to the top 11 finalists, and my play was one of the 11 selected. Therefore, I was invited to go up to New York, where they would do readings of my play along with the plays of 10 other teens, and from there they would select the top five.

The play I had written was called *Buddies*. The storyline, which takes place in DC, was about three teenagers who spent their extra time going to the go-gos, dealing with relationships with their girlfriends, and working through storms of tragedy that one of them had become involved in. The characters in the play were loosely based on people that I knew. For example, there was a teacher in the play that I based on CUE's founder Mrs. Johnson.

I'm not exactly sure what it was about the play that got it chosen as one of the top 11 finalists, but I always assumed that one of the main attractions that caught their attention about it was it was based on a black culture in the Washington, DC area. And out of all of the 11 finalists, it was the only one of that type. In truth, each of the 11 finalists represented their own totally different culture.

This trip to New York was going to be my first time ever leaving the area by myself, as well as my first time ever flying on an airplane. All the accommodations, including my flight, room, and food, had been set up for me. I was going to stay at Gerald Chapman's house, the director of the Young Playwrights Festival, for the first night, and then meet the director of my play and stay with her for the rest of the two weeks.

Also, being that it was my first time ever in New York by myself, I had no idea of the city. With the directions that my mom had written down and given me, I exited the plane at LaGuardia Airport and got into a taxicab. Based on those directions, I told the cab driver the address.

Apparently, my mom had never been to New York either, because the address they had given her over the phone was a destination that was located in Greenwich Village. However, the address that she had written down and given to me was written as *"Grinich" Village.* We reached that location around 1 o'clock in the morning, so it was dark. As I was about to step out of the cab, I noticed that the name on the street sign was different from the name that my mom had written. Not having a clue about New York at the time, I knew that the last thing I wanted was to be stranded and lost on some empty street at 1 o'clock in morning. I showed the cab driver the directions written by my mom, and I said to him, "No. I want to go to Grinich Village. This street sign says 'Greenwich' Village."

Immediately realizing my ignorance of the area, the cab driver replied, "Ohhhhhhh, Grinich Village!" And for the next hour and a half he drove me around New York City pretending to be looking for a street that he knew didn't exist.

Finally, I asked him to pull over to a pay phone so that I could call Gerald so he could help us out. That was when I found out the misspelling of Greenwich, and when Gerald realized the cab driver had taken advantage of my lack of knowledge of the city. The original address that we reached an hour and a half ago was, indeed, the correct address after all. Lesson learned.

The next day, I headed over to the theatre, which was located Off-Broadway, to meet with the other contestants in the competition, as well as the director and cast members who would be doing the reading of my play. The person that was selected to direct my play was a woman who went by the name of Billie Allen. From that point on, it was Billie who took me under her wing and broke down the entire process that would be taking place.

She explained that the different actors and actresses whom she had selected for my play were all young, up-and-coming performers, all in their mid to late 20's, who at that point were not widely known, but were promising in the industry. Little did I know at the time just how promising they would end up.

One was a guy named Michael Wright, who, at the time, was just an aspiring actor with lots of talent, but less than 10 years later became pretty famous from acting in movies such as *Streamers* and *Sugar Hill*. His most popular role was the character Eddie King, Jr. in The Five Heartbeats.

Another cast member was a woman by the name of Anna-Marie Horsford. She was cast to play the role of Mrs. Johnson. Again, although she was an up-and-coming actress at the time, she ended up becoming a recognizable face in the industry about 5 years later for her role in a TV comedy series with Sherman Hemsley called *Amen*. She then became highly recognized as Ice Cube's mother in the movies *Friday* and *Friday After Next*. She then starred as a security guard full of personality in the TV comedy series *The Wayans Brothers*.

There was also another young, up-and-coming actress who went by the name of Kim Western-Moran. Just like Billie Allen, Kim took it upon herself to take me under her wing while I visited New York. She would take me to the different places in the city and school me on the dos and don'ts of how to maneuver. At the time, Kim was also working on another play, which was actually one of my favorites called *A Raisin in the Sun*, and she would take me with her when she rehearsed. It was at her rehearsal that I met another actress by the name of Phylicia Ayres-Allen (later known as Phylicia Rashad), who became a household name less than a year later from her role as Claire Huxtable on *The Cosby Show*.

Phylicia Rashad was so cool to me. When Kim introduced me to the cast, explaining to them who I was and about the Young Playwright's Festival that I had come to New York for, Phylicia showed the most interest. She gave me a welcoming smile, shook my hand, and welcomed me to the world of theatre. She was a pleasure to be around. I sat to the side and observed their rehearsals, and she even was courteous to the point where she would ask if I was doing okay.

The actor who Billie had chosen to play the main character in my play was a young, debonair actor that had talent dripping from him. He was clearly everyone's favorite, and, as a matter of fact, Billie preached and predicted to me how she felt he was going to be a big actor one day, and she was actually right about that. His name was Denzel Washington, and he had yet to do any movies, but he was well known on the theater circuit.

Denzel brought more life to the character he portrayed than I envisioned when I created the character. In certain scenes he portrayed the character as I wrote him, while in others he went in a different direction that pulled people in emotionally. For example, instead of getting the impression that the character was just angry, he would deliver it in a way where you also felt sorry for him, which gave it structure and more understanding as to why the character was doing the things that he was doing.

What really caught my attention, something I really appreciated and respected of Denzel, was how he asked my opinion on the character before taking him in a particular direction. It didn't take long before I realized he was everything Billie boasted about. He was the truth.

Denzel came to every rehearsal wearing a high school letterman jacket, and on the chest of it were the words *A Soldier's Story* in cursive. Whenever he and I sat around and talked about the character, the script or anything else, I agreed with much of what he said because he was sharp, skillful, and brilliant. As a student in the game, I found myself learning a lot simply by engaging in conversation with him. Not only did Denzel bring deeper meaning and depth to the character and the story, he took my understanding of acting to a higher level by showing me the depth an actor can go to actually become the character. Denzel also brought Charles Fuller to a reading and introduced him to all of us. He is the man who wrote both *A Soldier's Story* and the original *A Soldier's Play*. About a year later, the world witnessed Denzel's brilliance in his first major acting role as the movie *A Soldier's Story* hit theaters, and that's when I figured out the jacket he wore every day had much more meaning than I thought.

Each and every day for the next two weeks, we gathered in that theatre. They rehearsed the play, while I watched intently. If there were any changes or updates that needed to be made in the script, I would spend my nights rewriting them, and then the next day we would rehearse the changes.

To help with the cultural understanding of my play, there was a lot of information we shared and discussed about each other. They explained to me their lifestyles and the psychology behind a New York state of mind, and I described to them all the intricate details about the DC area's music called Go-Go. Since Go-Go music was mentioned and talked about frequently within my play, they needed to be able to develop an understanding as to exactly what it was. Other than Chuck Brown's "Bustin' Loose" and Trouble Funk's "Pump Me Up," which were radio-friendly studio versions of what Go-Go actually was, they did not know anything about the culture, and they surely never heard the term "Go-Go." I had to describe to them exactly what the experience and event were like, and the only way I could do that at the time was play for them some of my PA tapes of other groups such as Rare Essence, EU, Ayre Rayde, and

Mass Extinction. I did everything I could to help them understand what the live experience of Go-Go sounded and felt like.

At the end of the readings and two weeks in New York, I was told they were going to have another breakdown, and then they were going to choose the best 5 reading performances from the 11 presented. Just like before, they would contact me and let me know if my play was chosen as one of the final 5.

Three months later, they called me again, and I was right back out there as one of the top 5 finalists, and I was working with the same director and cast members. This time, out of the final 5 selected, they were going to select the best one and do a full production Off-Broadway of it.

Although I did not make it as the final winner, that part didn't even matter to me because I didn't even expect to get as far as I did. When I wrote and sent the play in, what I expected to get from them was their promise to at least critique it. Needless to say, those two trips spent in New York rehearsing, learning, networking, and finally being able to watch a stage presentation of something that I had written, were moments that trumped most of my life experiences to that point. Here I was a 17-year-old kid just sitting back and absorbing everything. If I was different when I returned back to the neighborhood from spending time at Duke Ellington, I was definitely a whole different person after spending that time in New York.

For a considerable amount of time, I was in a world that I had always dreamed about being part of. Yes, that was the type of dream that every child had, but the difference was that not every child got to experience and absorb the realities of that dream. Consequently as they grow older, their realization of the truths of reality and the world slowly takes over and crushes their dreams. That was the moment I understood that in order for a child to make it out of the neighborhood, the child has to believe there are more things other than the neighborhood; and not only does the child have to believe it, it has to experience and see it for itself. I considered myself blessed to have been able to do that, and I understood and realized that I'd seen and experienced things that others in my neighborhood had not nor had a clue of their possibilities. There's no question that a child's horizons can be broadened with each and every new experience of scenery and cultures they get the opportunity to experience.

THE HOWARD THEATRE

The people that I met and the connections that I made during my time in New York actually turned out to be a benefit for me when I returned to Maryland. At times whenever I got bored or found myself yearning to work in a theatrical environment, I could call up to New York to someone such as Gerald Chapman or Billie Allen, and they would connect me with some temporary work with some of the theatres in DC such as Arena Stage.

I started to mature and realize that whenever I was not busy doing something positive, negative people and situations were right there. The less that I was involved in some type of music or theater event, the more I was slowly finding myself hanging with the guys in the neighborhood and slowly getting into trouble. I began doing the same senseless things that I was doing before I got into Duke Ellington. Since going to the go-go was the single thing I enjoyed doing besides working in CUE and spending time with my girlfriend, the things that I would get myself in trouble doing basically involved figuring out ways to get money in order to be able to go to the go-go.

Not having enough money in our pockets for admission to see Rare Essence play at The Howard Theatre every Friday night, we would do mischievous things to get money. At the time, going to see a band at The Howard Theatre would only cost five dollars.

For example, during the week when my mom would give me a dollar for lunch money, instead of using it to buy lunch, I would pocket it, sneak through the lunch line, and steal my lunch. By the time Friday night rolled around, I would end up with a total of five dollars saved from that week.

Actually, the mood of the Howard Theatre started earlier that day in school. The dialogues by seventh period would go like this:

"Are you going tonight?"

"Who's playing?"

"I think it's supposed to be Petworth, Pump Blenders, and Rare Essence."

"Yeah, I'm going. Who are you riding up there with?"

"I don't know yet. I'm rolling with whatever crew is heading in that direction."

"Sho ya right."

By night time, a bunch of us in the neighborhood would gather together and gamble for money by holding crap games (Rolling dice). For some of us, the purpose for getting into the crap game was to be able to have more money to go to The Howard Theatre later that night. If we lost in the crap game, that meant we weren't going anywhere. And, of course, if we won, The Howard Theatre was the next destination. From there we would walk up to the district line and catch the X2 metro bus to The Howard. Then after spending practically the entire night there, we would head back outside just as the morning sun was coming up and jump on the metro to head home. That was our routine every Friday, but the initial five dollars is what I needed to begin.

Now it really wasn't too much of a big deal if you ended up going there alone because you were surely going to run into some of your hangout buddies once you got there. This was where everybody was anyway.

The line going into The Howard was another story of its own. Wrapped around the side of the building there were two types of patrons: the ones who were eager to get inside, and the ones who just waited and hung outside until it was time for Rare Essence to hit the stage. The latter of the two would have to hang somewhere across the street or kick it for a while on Georgia Avenue because of Officer Robinson. He was a tall, black man who walked around swinging his Billy club, and he wasn't having crowds just gather in front of The Howard on his watch. And if you planned to go inside, you'd better make sure that you were in line or else. Once inside, you were attacked by the DJ record spins and wizardry vocals of Tricky Rick ("the trickiest man in town").

There were crews all over the place. "Crews" is the term we used for large groups of people, and they were normally from the same area. Some within the crew came for the music, some came for the girls, and some came ready to fight. The A-Team and the Hill Boys had their designated sections on the balcony. The Gangsta Chronicles dominated most of the seats near the camera stand (Some of the names make it obvious we watched a lot of television back then). South East, 7th and T, Sursom Corda, Montana Avenue, and even parts of Maryland such as Seat Pleasant, Landover, Suitland, and Oxon Hill had their mobs up in the place. Tricky Rick acknowledged them all. He must have known every single person in the place.

Although waiting for the bands to set up took what seemed like an eternity, their shows were worth the wait. You could always tell when the last band was ready and about to play (besides the fact that it was about 3 in the morning) because the lights would go down. Not only that, but the tone in Tricky Rick's conversation would slowly but surely begin to echo. This scene caused everyone to gracefully trickle down towards the stage. Tricky Rick's introduction of the bands were like a game show emcee that enthusiastically "psyche" up the crowd before even mentioning the band's name. It would go something like this:

"Now, we're ready to rock your SOCKS-SOCKS-SOCKS!
To make your dreams come TRUE-TRUE-TRUE-TRUE!
As we make your bodies MOVE-MOVE-MOVE-MOVE!
With DC's total GROOVE-GROOVE-GROOVE!
The only ones to make your bodies MOVE-MOVE-MOVE!
HERE - IS - RARE........Essssssssssssssence-sence-sence-sence!"

In fact, by the time he got to the band's name, they would have already started and have been well into a strong pocket (a tight, steady groove) before Tricky Rick's famous echo ended. He always set the party off, and the folks who lingered outside were now fighting to get in.

This was also during the first and very last time that I actually experimented with the drug called "Lovely," referred to on the streets as "Love Boat." It was on a Friday night, and we were just standing with some friends on 7th & T getting ready to head into The Howard. One of the guys pulled out a small piece of aluminum foil and rolled the contents up in some Top paper. Although it looked like a marijuana joint, it was much smaller in depth, and it definitely did not smell like a regular marijuana joint. It had a really awful chemical smell to it. I knew exactly what it was, but I never tried it before. And although I was never really even a big weed smoker, as the guys began passing it around, I took two small hits off of it anyway.

At first I felt absolutely nothing. I even made a comment about how weak it was, but as I took my first step to head into The Howard, the high hit me immediately like a ton of bricks. It didn't just gradually sneak up on me the way weed did, it hit me all at once as soon as I took that first step. For the rest of that night, all I could think about was how I couldn't wait for that high to come down. I don't even remember much of what the band played that night. The only thing that I took notice to was the fact that when you are high off of Love Boat, you can immediately identify everyone else in the room who is high off of it as well because they all look like exactly how you feel, and they're all saying the same things that you are saying, "I swear I ain't never smoking this shit again."

Although I've heard many people say that before and end up doing it again and again, I truly meant it. There was nothing about it whatsoever that I liked, especially the smell of it. It seemed to have lingered on me the entire night.

I should have known better anyway. The few times that I smoked weed always ended up as unenjoyable experiences. In the beginning, I always felt smoking weed was a good thing because, for some reason, I could hear music more clearly while high. I would always put in some type of PA tape of a Go-Go band, or something from Maze featuring Frankie Beverly, and I could hear every single instrument that was being played. I would just be in a zone listening to that music and hearing things that I had not originally noticed whenever I listened to it before I got high.

Eventually, being high caused me to think too much, and thinking too many things at one time can be dangerous. At least for me it was. Every time I smoked weed and began thinking too much, I started realizing just how much I was fucking up. Then I would get depressed about what I was doing. I'd repeat to myself over and over again, "Man, I'm fucking up like shit. I'm fucking up like shit." I definitely should have known better than to hit that Love Boat, but being young and dumb, those were the kinds of things I found myself getting involved with while hanging with some of the guys around the neighborhood.

One night as we were heading out to catch the metro bus to the go-go, we had come up with the idea that it would be a better night if we actually were able to drive to the go-go instead. So on our route, we spotted a woman walking towards her car and decided that we were going to rob her.

Slowly the three of us crept up on the woman as she was opening her car door. She turned around and fearfully began explaining to us that she did not have any money, but we went through her pockets, purse, and car anyway. Finally, after realizing that she indeed did not have any money, we started walking away. That's when something made me remember just how close to a police station we were. I said to the guys, "We're going to have to take her car because if we try to walk back home, she can easily just drive to the police station and they could just grab us before even making it home."

Eager to be able to have a car, they immediately ran back towards her. The woman began crying and asking us not to take her car, but we took it anyway. The plan I had come up with was to take the car, drive it to a neighborhood that was closer to ours, park it with the keys left inside, and walk through the woods to get home. That way, eventually they would find the car, she would get it back undamaged, and we would already be home safely without being arrested. No harm. No foul. No conviction.

Just like I explained it to them, we left the car and keys in the adjacent neighborhood and headed home. However, halfway into the woods, the other two guys must have got the feeling that everything was safe and we were in the clear because they decided they were going to go back and get the car. My not wanting to be part of it, as well as not wanting to take the woman's car and do whatever with it, I decided that I was not going to go back with them. I proceeded home.

By the time I reached the other end of the woods just across the road from where we lived, I noticed flashing police lights at a distance up the road. Taking a closer look, I realized that the car the guys decided to go back and get was pulled over by the police. I swiftly dashed across the highway and headed home. For the rest of the night, I sat in my room with mixed thoughts about many things. I could not get out of my head the horrible vision of the woman crying as we took her car, and the thought of my two buddies being pulled over and arrested by the police. Even more frightening to me was the feeling that at any minute the police would be knocking on my door because my buddies would surely tell them that I was the third person that stole the car. I was restless and nervous as hell, and the whole time I was thinking over and over again, *I'm fucking up like shit.*

Needless to say, the police never did come to my house because they never told the police that I was with them. That was when I realized I had gone too far, so I made a phone call to New York. My contacting the people I had come to know there was basically my cry for help. I knew that if I had kept on the road that I was traveling, I was going to end up either in jail or dead. I knew it. I was fucking up like shit, and this time I didn't need the weed to tell me so.

GETTING BACK INTO FOCUS

One of the biggest things that I was able to generate from my connection with New York was the opportunity to be able to put on my play here in DC. This was something that was able to keep me very busy, hence keep me from continuing to do stupid things.

Re-connecting with some of my friends from Duke Ellington, we applied for and were awarded a grant that allowed us to perform my play at the Eastern Market Gallery. Due to us still being age qualified to again work under the Marion Barry Summer Youth Employment Program, we were able to get paid while doing so. Thus, every day for that summer our job was rehearsing for the play *Buddies* that I had written. And then once production was finally completed, put on the play at Eastern Market Gallery.

While at a regular family gathering at my grandmother's house, I noticed my cousin Byron was not there. I asked his sister Kia where he was, and she told me that he was now playing with Rare Essence. He wouldn't be coming to the family gathering because he had a show with them that evening. I almost fell out of my chair. The same musician that I looked up to for his musical talent and gifts since I was a little boy was now playing with a band that I always looked up to. This excited the hell out of me. The fact that he was my cousin was the icing on the cake. What better feeling could one have than going to see the one musician he was always inspired by, performing on the same stage with the one band he was always inspired by? I immediately contacted him the next day and asked if I could ride to some of their shows with him. I knew this would allow me to learn even more about music.

During the day, I would rehearse for the play, and at nights when Rare Essence played, Byron would let my little brother Chucky and me go with him to the shows. One of the regular spots that we would hit with Byron would be a club called The Room, which was located in the heart of Downtown DC. The difference with my going to see Rare Essence this time, as opposed to the other times I would go, was that because I was there with Byron, I was sort of like on the inside of things when it came to being up close and personal to the band's interactions with each other. Because of this, I started to get to know some of the members personally. This set my being able to watch and observe them while playing from a whole different angle and perspective.

Another thing about being able to ride to the shows with Byron is that often times I got to see the band's performances from the other side of the stage as opposed to standing in the crowd. I would stand behind the band where I not only was able to watch the band as a whole execute their songs, but also see the individual cues and stage communication between the members.

One of my favorite places to stand was directly behind Footz on the drums. Since the drummer is usually the driving force of a band and the main individual who is continually in motion throughout the entire set, it was always interesting watching Footz in action. His timing was like clockwork. I don't think I've ever seen him miss a beat or a cue.

In fact, I would be amazed watching the entire backline from that view because Footz and the conga player Go-Go Mickey would be joking and clowning around. I thought Footz was surely going to miss a cue from the front line, but no matter how much he and Mickey joked and played around, whenever anything was called, he was right on cue, never missing a beat. Although there were other phenomenal drummers on the circuit such as Sugar Foot Ricky, JuJu House, and Mack from Trouble Funk that were superior in other genres, there was no question that when it came to the genre of Go-Go, Footz was the tightest.

Whereas many of the other drummers fancied themselves with dazzling showmanship of drum rolls, rudiments, and breakdowns on the drum sets, I gravitated to the way Footz delivered his. He did long and subtle drum rolls that were always in timing, never throwing anything offbeat, never out of sync, and never out of the pocket. His timing was impeccable.

Funky Ned, who was the bass guitar player of Rare Essence, was another artist I enjoyed watching. Just like Footz, hearing him from the crowd or through a PA tape was one thing, but watching him in action up close was a whole different story. His skill and artistry on the strings was amazing. Watching him work the bass guitar was always interesting and entertaining.

There was a young house DJ at The Room who went by the name of DJ Kool. Because of The Room, next to Tricky Rick, he began to become one my favorite DJs that spun at go-gos. The difference between his style and Tricky Rick's style was that even though DJ Kool did not exactly have that charismatic personality that made Tricky Rick so popular, the style in which he mixed records was phenomenal to watch. Whereas Tricky Rick just played records and talked to the crowd, DJ Kool was a wizard with scratching records, and especially mixing them. He had a style where he would just jump back and forth, and back and forth again, from one turntable to the other mixing the songs together.

One night while Rare Essence was taking a break, DJ Kool, who was playing records as he always did, called out to Little Benny on the mic and asked who wrote their song "Body Moves." Benny replied to him that "Body Moves" was actually written and produced by Chuck Brown.

Before the band was about to take the stage and begin their second set, DJ Kool put on the record "Body Moves." As Benny, Whiteboy, Funky Ned, Footz, Godfava, Markie, GoGo Mickey, and David

Green began picking up their instruments, they started playing alongside the record. Before anyone in the crowd realized what was happening, DJ Kool had gradually turned the volume of his turntables all the way down, and the band was fully into the song without missing a single beat. If you had not been watching them in action, you would not have even realized that it actually happened at all. You would just be wondering, *Damn, when did the band start playing?* It was just that smooth. It is still one of the slickest ways I have ever seen any band take the stage.

As if all that wasn't enough, another thing that had taken place while at Bowie High School was that I started practicing with other musicians in the neighborhood again in attempt to start another band. I was working out with a group of guys from Seat Pleasant, and a friend from school named David Powell had a band from Washington Heights. Eventually the two of us merged together calling ourselves Pure Elegance. Although we had not started playing any shows yet, we were practicing together heavily in order to reach a point of being good enough to do so.

1985-1987

BOWIE STATE

It took what seemed to be an eternity, along with the help of a miracle or two, but finally I accumulated enough credits to be able to graduate from high school. I considered this a miracle because I almost didn't get the credits at all. When I found out that I was two credits short from being able to graduate, I was fed up and tired of the whole thing. I was just going to drop out and say forget it all, but the assistant principal there, a woman who had taken a liking to me, called me privately into her office. She began talking to me and explaining how important school was and why I should come back for another half of year to get those two credits. After her talk, I decided to take her advice. Biting the bullet of the embarrassment of having to return after the summer was over, I went back to school that fall for only half of a year and I got my two credits.

Now during my entire time in high school, if anyone would've asked me if I was planning on going to college, my answer was a definite "No." I had no desire whatsoever to continue school once I finally got out of school. I had not given college a thought ever before in life, but by the time I was approaching graduation, a wild thing happened. Because of the many actions and accomplishments in accordance with my affiliation with Street Theater, going to Duke Ellington, writing the play, and having a production of the reading in New York, and even being able to do a production of that same play here in DC, I was encouraged by my sister and my godmother, Mrs. Bernice Mann of Beulah Baptist Church, to go ahead and try to apply for this Maryland State Scholarship that was available for theater.

In order to be able to be considered to win this scholarship, you had to audition two theatre monologues. One had to be from any traditional play, and the other had to be a Shakespeare piece. Having done this a few times before, this was all familiar territory for me.

The two pieces that I decided to audition with were from *A Raisin in the Sun* and Shakespeare's *Othello*. By the time all was said and done, I passed the audition and won the Maryland State Scholarship award for theater. I started going to Bowie State College that spring. As a matter of fact, I didn't even go to my high school graduation because the excitement for me doing that passed away. I literally went straight from being a student at Bowie High School one week, to a student at Bowie State College the next. It was just that quick.

GOOD TO GO

While living on campus at Bowie State, I had gotten the word of a casting call for a movie that was being made in DC about Go-Go music. My buddy Chuck Byrd, from the TNT Poppers and Duke Ellington, and I decided to go down there together and audition. The auditions took place on the campus of Howard University. By the time we got there, tons of people were already lined up waiting to get in. We were told that they were looking for people to play different types of roles, and the ones that we fit the description of were basically street, rugged, thug characters in DC crews. The audition monologue piece that I decided to use was actually a piece from the play I had written. By the time I took the stage and finished my audition piece, I received really good nods from the panel, giving me the impression that most likely I would be considered for a role. They told me that if I was considered, I would be hearing from them within the next two weeks. The movie was going to be called Good to Go, which was actually taken from a popular saying in the area during that time.

Ultimately, I never did receive that call, or at least I thought I didn't. I later found out that they had indeed called me, it's just that I was never given the message. You see, at the time I was living on campus at Bowie State in a dorm called Holmes Hall. There were no phones in our dorm rooms, but there was a pay phone on each floor of the building. Therefore, usually if anyone in any of the dorm rooms would hear the phone ring, they would go answer it and then go to the particular dorm room of the person receiving the call to let them know that there was a phone call waiting for them. Apparently, either I was not in my dorm at the time they called me, or whoever received the call just decided not to bother to come and get me, nor give me the message. Either way, I missed the opportunity to be in the movie, which now that I look back, I guess you can say that I actually dodged a bullet.

However, my man Chuck did receive the call, and was indeed cast in the movie as a gang member. As a matter of fact, a whole bunch of people I went to school with from Duke Ellington were cast in the movie including one of my theater teachers Linda Gravatt. And due to the fact that Chuck had been cast, I was actually privy to a lot of information pertaining to the process of the making of this movie.

I got to read the script, and something about the movie just did not make any sense. First of all, it was written by a guy from London, England named Blaine Novak. That part alone told me that either he spent a lot of time within the Go-Go community and culture, or that he was receiving third-party information regarding the ongoing activities that took place within the Go-Go community and culture. Nevertheless, it wasn't just that which threw me off from it, there were a lot of things that were written in the script that didn't make any sense to me, or rather wasn't an accurate description of what I knew Go-Go to be. For example, there was one particular scene in the script where Go-Go impresario Maxx Kidd, played by actor Robert DoQui, was explaining to some reporters what Go-Go is. In his explanation he basically stated, "Well, when you go, you like to go. And because you like to go, you like to Go-Go."

We used to get a big kick out of reading that, as well as many other things that were written in the script because they were corny and definitely out of touch. They were all too funny to us, but this was a movie that was going to be made and shown in theaters nationally. To us, that was a good look in many ways: a good look for Chuck to add to his resume, and a good look for Go-Go to finally get the national attention that it deserved.

Another point was how Chuck was actually cast in the first place. You see, he was actually chosen later after another guy from Duke Ellington's art department dropped out. When he had gotten the call to come out and audition for the second time, he was given the impression that he was going to be cast as the gang leader because that was the part he was given the second time to read, but when asked what part he was auditioning for, he told them the role of the gang leader. They told him that role was already filled by an upcoming actor name Fred Brathwaite (later to be known as Fab Five Freddy of *Yo! MTV Raps*). To us, that appeared to be a sign of being unorganized. That was something that we weren't used to because we were always used to doing our own thing and being on point about it such as the production we put on at the Eastern Market Gallery.

I would also go with Chuck when he was shooting many of the scenes for the movie, which always seemed to take place at night. On the times when he was not working on the movie, we would go together to watch as they shot other scenes such as when they would record live scenes of bands playing. These scenes were filmed at the old Post Office building located in downtown DC, and would actually be opened to the public for the purpose of generating an audience atmosphere for the bands while they were shooting. The bands that they were filming at these times were Redds and The Boys, who this story somewhat wrapped around, and Trouble Funk.

Although I was not in the area when the movie did finally hit the theaters, I received word that it actually turned out to be a flop. I saw it years later and, just as I read in the script, with the exception of the actual Go-Go bands and the scenes that took place inside of the go-go, everything else was basically Hollywood fluff, and it was over the top with everything that it was supposed to depict about culture in DC.

The characters of the gang members, who I assume were supposed to depict the life and styles of the different crews in the area such as the A-Team, Hillboys, and Gangster Chronicles, actually looked, dressed, and acted like they were gang members from the Kurt Russell movie *Escape from New York*.

The movie starred a person who had to have been the most boring person in the history of Hollywood cinematography — Art Garfunkel. Who knows, maybe if they cast someone else more energetic and exciting in that role, it could've been a little better.

The biggest disappointment and shock that really turned everyone off was a scene of a woman that was actually played by my teacher Linda Gravatt. In this scene, Linda is sitting at a bus stop at night waiting for the metro bus. Along came the gang members looking like they just came from a battle at the Terror Dome and attacks, rapes, and kills her. This was such a tasteless scene for many reasons, the main being the fact that a similar incident recently happened in the area. The sensationalizing of it in the movie did nothing but outrage people, and rightfully so. Instead of seeing a movie about Go-Go bands, this movie turned out to be about Hollywood-tized gang murder, police corruption, and a white hero who saves the day for Go-Go music and its culture. It definitely was not a good depiction of the culture that I had grown up in and loved.

The movie ranked as such a horrid mess that director Blaine Novak actually took his name off the credit of the movie as director and replaced it with the name Alan Smithe. This was a name that directors used when their movies were flops and they did not want their name to be attached to it any longer. The name of the movie was also changed from *Good to Go* to *Short Fuse*. Because of the failure of the movie, which was shown to a national audience, many felt that instead of shining a bright light of the Go-Go music scene to the world, it actually helped put a black eye on it.

The only positive that was gained by the movie was the soundtrack because of the bands who were on it. The movie promoted a song that was made by Redds and The Boys called "Movin' & Groovin'." That sprung as a number one hit, along with the video that accompanied it. The other song was a cut by Trouble Funk called "Still Smokin'," which actually became a hit, too.

LOVE

Love can make you do some things that you normally would not do. I am a witness to it and can testify to that notion.

Like just about every teenager, I fell in love for the first time during high school. I've had many girlfriends coming up, but when it came to my first love, the others were no comparison. And no question about it, you definitely know it when it hits you, and I was hit hard by it. With that being the case, it should come as no surprise that some of the major abrupt decisions that I have made in my life have actually been based on a current relationship of that time.

For example, the high school sweetheart that I had a crush on was another factor that played a part of my realizing just how much I was messing up while at Bowie High School. Her name was Judy, and I first met her in the school cafeteria. She was sitting at a table with some of her friends, and I was sitting at a table with some of mine. I saw her across the room and she immediately caught my attention. She was just cute as a button to me, so in my attempt to try to get her attention, I started throwing raisins at her. As juvenile as this may have been, it did create an opportunity for me to strike up a conversation with her. Even though that conversation consisted of my explaining to her why I was throwing raisins at her, at least my foot was in the door.

For the remainder of my high school years, she was the one for me. We were basically inseparable. Just as any other high school couple, we did just about everything together. We shared lockers together, met in between classes and passed notes to each other, and we talked about our dreams and desires. To top it all off, the girl could sing. To me, that was the icing on the cake. During times we spent alone, I would enjoy just sitting back and listening to her sing to me. I loved hearing her sing anything by Teena Marie. Judy would sing songs such as "Dear Lover" and "Stop The World," and would sound exactly like Teena Marie. As a matter of fact, Teena Marie became our personal favorite when it came to music that was shared only between us.

When I would go to the Pure Elegance band practice sessions, it was Judy who I couldn't wait to get home and tell about how things went that night. The same thing went with the things that I was doing with CUE and any and everything else that I was involved in. Without a doubt, she was my muse, and you almost never saw one of us without seeing the other. We were going together very strong, but also just like any young couple, we had our falling out times, our breaking up times, and our getting back together times.

When I started going to Bowie State, we were in one of our getting back together times. This time we're coming back together from a longer hiatus than normal, and since I was out of high school and a little wiser and more mature, things with us had gotten stronger than ever before. This time, we began talking and putting plans together towards actually getting married. The only problem was the fact that I had no money, no plans, and no future to be talking about marrying anyone. The only thing I had that was of any value was my guitar, and the only value that had was due to my personal sentiments. That was when I woke up one morning and made what had to have been probably one of the craziest decisions that I had ever made in my life — I enlisted in the US Army. My rationale for this was to have a sure thing in regards to building a nest egg for a family.

Of course, something like this would put an immediate hold on anything else that I had going on. In fact when it came to Bowie State, I never even dropped out. I just simply left without saying anything to them. That was just how fast I always jumped into things. Once I made up my mind that I wanted to do something that I strongly felt was worth doing, I shot for it, and Judy was worth that to me.

Maybe the Army recruiter sensed the same thing about me because he scheduled to send me away two weeks from the date of my signing up. I officially had 14 days to do whatever I needed to do before being in the Army.

The night before leaving for the Army, I was able to squeeze in one more night of Go-Go. My cousin Byron took me with him for his performance with Rare Essence at Crystal Skate. He let everyone in the band know I was scheduled to leave for the Army the next morning, so that was an unofficial going away party. I was even able to chill on the stage behind Footz on the drums throughout the entire show one more time. Their entire performance was more than enough to set my spirit correctly in a Go-Go zone as I flew to El Paso, Texas a few hours after the show.

I was standing in formation on a cold November morning along with a whole bunch of other new recruits at Fort Bliss, El Paso, Texas, desperately trying to figure out what in the hell had I gotten myself into this time. It was just that quick. Too much of an abrupt change!

IN THE ARMY NOW

And just that quickly, I had come to the realization that maybe I made a mistake here. Immediately my mind started thinking back on some of my friends who tried to talk me out of going, but by this time it was too late. I was already there, I had sworn in, and the changing my mind thing was something that the Army did not play. Once you're sworn in, you will commit to it or go to jail. There was no turning back, so the only thing that I could do was try to make the best of what I was now involved with.

At the same time, part of me also felt that this was a good move because it was still a plan towards my future with Judy. And after a while, I started getting used to my new settings. I was even designated to be platoon leader. This was a position that allowed me to be the lead when we would march and do our cadence. In fact, I actually became popular in my platoon for leading the cadence calls. Therefore as we marched to our different designations, I would be the one to lead the songs that we sang.

Eventually after the basic training part of it was over, we were able to have access to our personal belongings. Being able to have my guitar actually served as a soothing method for me during AIT, which is the second level of basic training. I was able to zone out from there, and zone in to my guitar.

After spending several months going through basic training and then AIT, I was shipped to Kitzingen, Germany, where I was assigned to Larson Barricks. My arrival to Germany turned out to be a horror story of its own because my luggage was lost when I got there. I made it to Germany safely, but my luggage never got there at all.

Basically what happened was when boarding the plane in Texas to fly to Germany, I was only able to carry on two pieces of my luggage on the flight. The two pieces that I chose were my guitar and another smaller bag that contained all of my Go-Go PA tapes. Everything else had to be stored under the plane with the luggage. Once I arrived in Frankfurt, Germany and went to the airport's baggage claim area to pick up the rest of my luggage, I discovered that my luggage never even got loaded onto the plane, and that meant I had nothing. All my clothes, shoes, and toiletries were gone. Needless to say, that started off my being in a whole different country at a low point.

I then had to travel from Frankfurt to Kitzingen where I was designated to sign in to the 3rd Infantry Division on Larson Barracks. Of course, I knew no one there, but one thing I did discover was a rec center on the premises. This place became my source of release. It consisted of music rooms where soldiers could reserve time spots and practice on many of the instruments already provided. Many of the rooms were large enough for an entire band to practice, and some were just small rooms where individuals could go and practice alone or record themselves if they wanted to. I definitely found myself engrossed in it, and would spend all of my time there once I was off duty. Of course, there were other military personnel who would be there jamming on their instruments, I began networking with many of them simply because of our interest in music. They became my new friends while in Germany.

In between doing my duty as a soldier and on my free time playing music at the rec center, the only other thing I looked forward to was receiving letters, mainly from Judy. Being over there in Germany in another country can actually be kind of depressing because a person is steadily wishing a whole lot to be back home in America. In Europe, we often referred to home as "The World." For example, a person would say, "Man, I can't wait to get back to The World." This would actually be them saying, "I can't wait to get back home to America."

Because it was a different culture in a different area with an entirely different language, everything over there was not for us. For example, television; unless you spoke German fluently, it didn't make any sense to watch TV. So unless you watched the one military channel that was available for us to watch, which was boring as hell, soldiers made a big deal in purchasing VCRs. That way they could watch videotapes of movies instead. Another thing that was good about that was you could contact somebody back in The World and have them send you television programs on videotape, and you definitely wanted to make sure that you told them to include the commercials and the news. Watching those things would give you the feeling of being at home.

Receiving letters from Judy, her brother George, and my brother Chucky, helped sustain me a whole lot over there. They not only sent letters, they would also send me copies of the latest PA tapes released on the Go-Go scene. By them doing that, I was actually able to keep up with what was happening in Go-Go without missing a beat. Also another cat who would send me PA tapes was a guy we called Richie Reds. I knew him from when I was working out with the band Pure Elegance, and Richie would always send me tapes of them since they started playing shows while I was gone.

One of the things they all informed me about was that Little Benny was no longer with Rare Essence. Apparently he and a few other members left the band and started their own, calling it Little Benny and The Masters.

With all these items being sent to me and keeping me upbeat, it wasn't too long before I began noticing a change in the regular routine. The letters that I was receiving from Judy weren't coming as frequently as they had been in the beginning. Unfortunately, it had gotten to the point where I basically stopped receiving any letters at all.

Finally, one day as I went to check my mail, I noticed a letter from her. Her letters were always easy to notice from a distance because the envelopes would always be colorful such as pink or light blue, but this time something didn't feel right about it. As I grabbed the letter heading out toward the rec center for another practice session, I began reading it. By the time I got to the middle of the letter, everything in my heart and soul just dropped. Indeed I had received what was widely known in the military as a "Dear John Letter." In other words, it was a letter that basically told me she had met a new man and began a new relationship with him. The only thing that I could think about was a cadence song that I used to sing while stationed in El Paso that goes, "Ain't no sense in going home, Jody's got your girl and gone." Now I don't know if her new boyfriend's name was Jody, but it was clear to me in black and white that he's definitely got her, and they were gone.

This horrible news sent me into a state of confusion and I felt more alone at that point than I ever felt before in my life. Here I was in the US Army, stationed thousands of miles away from home, and the main reason that I went over there in the first place no longer existed. Instead of going to the rec center, I immediately made a u-turn and headed back to my barracks. I wasn't in the mood to be playing any music.

After several days of just hanging around my barracks in such a depressed zone, I eventually started going back to the rec center to play my music. It was no doubt the only thing I felt that I had left, and the only thing left that I had that I was able to find solace in.

Getting back into my zone of playing my music, there was a band that practiced in one of the rooms at the rec center who called themselves Suave. They were considered one of the top bands at Larson, and every once in a while they would let me sit in on their practice sessions with my guitar. I happened to be sitting in during the time they were practicing for the USAEUR Battle of the Bands competition. This was an annual event held in Europe where acts from the military bases would come together to showcase their talents in hopes of qualifying for the All-Army Battle, which took place in the US. This was actually the same type of competition in DC that I was involved with while with the TNT Poppers, but the difference was the USAEUR competition consisted only of bands. Much like the competition in DC, it had levels. You would go to one level of the competition located in a particular area, and if you won, you would advance to the next level, which would take place at a different location a week later.

Since I had been working out with Suave at the rec center, they asked if I was interested in being in the competition with them. Of course, I was interested. What kind of question was that? This was the type of thing that made me feel like I was back in The World. The only difference was that Suave played R&B music, playing such songs as Ready For The World's "Oh Sheila!," Wham's "Careless Whisper," Slave's "Watching You," Kool & the Gang's "She's Fresh," and Prince's "Do Me Baby." Those were the songs that we performed in the Battle of the Bands.

Suave already won two rounds of the competition and was gearing up for the final two. Also, in addition to being able to fly back to The World and play, one of the biggest things about the USAEUR competition was that if you won the final round of the Battle of the Bands, your band from that point would spend the rest of their entire military time there touring Europe. That was one thing I really looked forward to and was hoping to be able to do.

Once we got to the event of the Battle of the Band's 3rd level, we won again, and therefore were advancing to the final level, which took place in Hanau, Germany. Unfortunately, even though we made it to the final round, we actually lost to a band who not only looked like Graham Central Station, but their lead singer sounded just like Larry Graham.

After returning to Larson barracks from performing the Battle of the Bands with Suave, I decided that I wanted to start a band of my own. I developed a little popularity in the barracks by playing with Suave, and that allowed me to step out on my own and have lots of people take notice and pay attention.

Don't get me wrong, I had nothing against playing with Suave. I loved every moment of playing with them, but there was something in me yearning to want to have a Go-Go band while being stationed there. One of the biggest reasons was because out of all the bands stationed there, none were Go-Go. In fact unless you were from the DC area, you had no idea what Go-Go even was, and I saw this as an opportunity to try and make a mark doing something different than what everyone else were doing.

The dilemma though was, once again, the majority of people there had no clue what Go-Go was. I was able to connect with two other guys who were from DC: a drummer who went by the name of Holmes, and a keyboard player who went by the name of Jackson. It's the military, so everyone is referred to by their last name.

Working out at the rec center, we began to start recruiting members for the Go-Go band, while keeping in mind that the mission was to get them to play a style that they never even heard of. During the practice sessions, I would bring in PA tapes of the bands back in DC and we would do what one may call study sessions where the musicians studied the exact way the songs were being executed on the tapes. The biggest thing that we wanted them to focus on was the percussion. Our percussion had to be strong, had to have drive, and had to be exciting and dynamic just as it is in Go-Go.

Eventually we did start playing, and the uniqueness in which we presented the songs did catch people's attention. Before long we were finding ourselves playing a lot in different parts of Germany, mostly on the different Army bases at the NCO clubs. It was definitely our unique style that got us those gigs. Although the style was not new to Holmes, Jackson, and me, it was definitely new to almost everyone else there, unless, of course, they were from the DC area. It was Go-Go.

With so much going on, which definitely helped take my mind off of my Dear John letter, I was definitely not prepared for what I was about to encounter. Things were starting to get a bit tense there as far as racial issues go, and, for some reason, I was finding myself involuntarily being caught up in a couple of situations that had nothing to do with me. I'm not exactly sure why I had become the new target, but I got the impression that it had a lot to do with the fact I had been gone playing with the bands with the USAERU Battle of the Bands competitions and now with the increased popularity that my new Go-Go band were generating. Many of the soldiers in my barracks resented me for that. They somehow felt that it was unfair that they had to continue military duty on a daily basis, and I was always on the road. The walls were slowly but surely beginning to close in on me, and eventually two so-called incidents happened while I was on guard duty.

The first incident was a fight that happened between a black guy who was a PFC (Private First Class), and a white guy who was a Ssgt (Staff Sergeant). The Ssgt, who was super drunk at the time, began talking racial smack to the PFC about just how much he could whoop his ass if he wanted to. They then decided to go into a private area down the hall so that they could fight it out. A few minutes later, I heard one of them calling for help. I jumped up from my desk and ran down the hall to find out what was going on. When I arrived, there was the Ssgt sprawled out on the floor, and his face was bruised and bloody. The PFC was nowhere to be found, but it was clear that the PFC beat the living daylights out of the Ssgt. I helped him up and brought him back to my guard post area.

Needless to say, when all was said and done, I got in trouble, too. Why? Well, they said that it was because I was on guard duty when it happened, but I know that it was because the racial tension in our unit was getting thicker and thicker. It wasn't really because I was on guard duty when it happened. The real reason I got in trouble was because a black PFC kicked the living shit out of a white Ssgt, and another black PFC was on guard duty when it happened — me.

The second incident, which was basically a setup resulting from the first incident, was a situation involving an M16 rifle and folks accusing me of trying to steal it, which made no fucking sense whatsoever. I mean, what in the heck would I be doing in the US Army located in Germany trying to steal an M16 rifle? I may not have been the sharpest kid on my block, but I damn sure wasn't the dumbest either. Eventually that craziness was let go, and the accusations were dropped. First of all, because of my MOS (Military Occupational Specialty), my weapon wasn't even an M16, it was a .45. I'm also thinking that they also realized how ridiculous that was. And without a doubt, I was definitely relieved about that. However, along with a few other incidents that took place, it let me know one thing — if I didn't figure out a way to get out of there and back home, I was going to end up one of two places, dead or in Mannheim, a US Army prison. It was getting that serious out there.

Luckily, I had an ace in the hole — my personal Monopoly get out of jail free card. When I first joined the army 2 years prior, I found out, while in El Paso Texas Basic Training, that I was too short for my MOS. As funny as that may sound, it was true. My MOS job title was 16S. That means that I was infantry, and it also means that alongside the .45 on my hip, my weapon was a Stinger, which was a very large missile launcher that's used by hoisting it on your shoulder, and its purpose was shooting down enemy aircraft.

What I found out was because of my height, if I were to fire a Stinger missile from my shoulder, the back-blast area would be too low to the ground, which would cause the back-blast of the launcher to shoot back up from the ground causing my back to be set on fire. This means that I was actually erroneously enlisted by the recruiter. However, what they told me in basic training was to not worry about it because I'd probably never fire a real one anyway. That was my ace in the hole. My get out of jail free card to use whenever I needed.

Well, with the craziness that was now brewing in my unit regarding the racial tension, there was no better time to use that ace in the hole than that moment. I went to the top offices and told them of my MOS and height dilemma. After measuring my actual height, they discovered that I was indeed right and gave me two choices. Either pick a new job or go home.

By the summer of 1987, I was back in the DC area, and there were two things that I immediately did when I got there: one was hook up with an old girlfriend from high school, and two was hook back up with the Go-Go band that I was playing with when I first left in 1985, which was Pure Elegance.

HOME AGAIN

Now that I was back home, the one thing that I had come to the conclusion of was I was no longer interested in acting. I just wanted to continue to play music with nothing else to consume my time. This was a decision I made before going into the Army. Even though I received the scholarship to attend Bowie State because of acting, in truth my passion just was not in it like it used to be. This could also be another reason why I was so willing to leave Bowie State.

This conclusion had actually come to me based on the experience of being able to put on our own production when we did my play at the Eastern Market Gallery. That left me with the frame of mind of not wanting to have to stand in line with 150 to 200 different people all auditioning for the same acting roles. Doing our own show at the Eastern Market Gallery spoiled me. It gave me the realization that in order to do something that you really want to do, and to be sure that it really gets done, you basically have to do it yourself. To me, going against several other people all trying to get chosen for the same role was just like buying a lottery ticket. Maybe it was even worse because at least with a lottery ticket, more than one person can have the same number and they would win, whereas only one person out of several would be chosen for a role. Another interesting aspect is not being selected for a role may not have had anything to do with your talent. The process of it was just humiliating to me, and because of the Eastern Market Gallery production, I developed the frame of mind that if we want to have something, we will build it ourselves.

Growing up in the music environment of my neighborhood and city showed me a whole different point of view. Opportunities to play in bands were plentiful. If you weren't able to get into a particular band that you wanted, you could simply just start your own. That's the same type of mind frame of doing our own play. My focus and energy towards doing any type of theater anymore diminished, which meant that my focus and yearning for playing music grew even stronger.

One of the first things I did when I got home was head to UDC to register for school. In doing so, I was very shocked when I was told by their staff that I was not eligible to use my G.I. Bill to pay for college because I had gotten out the Army earlier than I originally signed up for. Now there was no option for me but to find a job.

The first job I received was at a McDonald's, and that only lasted for two weeks. I'm surprised I was able to deal with their disrespect even that long. The next idea I came up with since I couldn't go to college full time was to take one specific career course at the Washington School for Secretaries. The school was being shown on television, so I registered there to learn about computers. After nine months of training, I finally graduated the course and was ready for what I considered the real working world. My goal was to get a job where I could wear a suit and tie.

With that mission being accomplished, there were two more major parts to my life: one was a brand new daughter named Krystina, and the other was I had gotten back with the band Pure Elegance, the guys I started playing with before I left for the Army.

PURE ELEGANCE

Since I was now a new member back into an old band, a lot changed with the band since I had been gone. They had begun playing shows around town and actually started developing a name for themselves, but my coming back actually served as a plus for them. I'm not sure if it had anything to do with my talent as a guitar player, or the simple fact that I provided a new practice spot for them, which at the time they were in search of.

At the time, my older brother and his family were living in a house owned by my Aunt Norlishia, which was located on 49th St., North East, DC. Since I was now living there with my brother and his family, he had given me permission to use the basement as a practice spot for Pure Elegance.

Now this was not just an ordinary house that we were in. Before my brother moved in, this house was where my grandmother, aunt, and cousins lived, and it actually served as the main gathering location for my entire family, which means my parents, siblings, 10 aunts and uncles, and almost 40 cousins were there for certain holidays and events. Growing up all of my life going to this house all the time meant it was very familiar and sentimental to me: the bedrooms upstairs, the open areas upstairs, the family room, basement, etc. Now this was the place where I opened the doors for Pure Elegance to practice.

Pure Elegance was a very musical band. We looked up to many of the older bands, but especially Rare Essence and Ayre Rayde. We kind of patterned many of the ways we executed songs towards their styles of playing. Just like Rare Essence, we would vamp into songs, and sometimes not fully go into them, depending on the crowd's reaction to the vamping. We played in many places such as the

Tip Top Club located in Bladensburg, Maryland, and the Pic Center located in Seat Pleasant, Maryland.

Dave Powell, who still remained the leader of the band, and I had become somewhat pretty close to the point where we stayed in constant communication. In fact, Dave hooked me up with the job where he was working at the time. This meant that we saw each other every single day even outside of practices and shows. We always discussed things pertaining to the band such as the songs we played and the directions we took them in. A lot of my ideas for how to execute particular songs were actually listened to and used by the band.

Just like every other band on the Go-Go circuit, we had our rival band — a band that we really enjoyed playing shows with in a friendly but competitive way. We were always trying to prove to each other who was the better band. Our rival was a band called Quality, which was led by a very charismatic lead talker who went by the name of Tip-Top Ty. Whenever Quality and Pure Elegance would play on the same card, many of them orchestrated by a popular promoter named Big Butch, you knew that you were going to get one hell of a show that night.

I recall one night we were scheduled to play with Quality at a firehouse located in Landover, Maryland. The show was scheduled to take place on Christmas Night, therefore we had no doubt that the place would be packed because everyone was home for the holidays. Our practice sessions gearing up for this particular show were intense. Every song we worked on and every transition from song to song we made were created particularly and meticulously for the purpose of punishing Quality in that battle.

Dave developed an idea to bring a horn section into the band, a saxophone player by the name of Rodney, and a trumpet player who went by the name of Ron. That was something they never had before, and we were only used to seeing horn sections with some of the bigger bands. On the night that this particular battle took place, we opened up strong because of the addition of the new horn section. They were able to add flavor in some of the songs we played such as Eric B and Rakim's "Move The Crowd." We were also able to open our show with dynamic intros. On this particular show, we came out with Earth, Wind & Fire's "In The Stone," and it was a powerful beginning that showcased the horns out in front.

Although Quality did not come out with such a strong opening as we did, they did come out with a slick gimmick — all of their members came in stepping, and all were wearing Santa Claus hats. As far as who won the battle by the end of the night, it depends on who you asked and if that person enjoyed the music over dance steps and Santa Claus hats. Either way, it set a strong tone for what turned out to be a successful night of Go-Go.

A LESSON IN BAND POLITICS

The new horn section addition to the band apparently gave Dave an even greater sense of direction for the band, and he was actually correct in his excitement of it. Not only did it add an even greater presence to our sound, but it also added a stronger presence to our front line. The only problem was he appeared to give them more value over the band than probably necessary. That actually was the beginning of a lot of conflict.

Apparently Ron, the trumpet player, was not particularly fond of my style of guitar playing. This was nothing that I was directly aware of. As a matter of fact, as far as I was concerned things were going great. I'm not necessarily sure if it was my style of guitar playing that he disliked or my sense of music direction in the way that I was formatting some of the songs we were playing. Either way, it was apparently a problem that I had no idea existed.

Since we were practicing in my brother's basement, the first sign that I detected that there may have been some type of problem brewing was an evening when practice was supposed to have taken place and not one member of the band showed up. What made it crazier was I did not receive a call from Dave or anyone stating that practice would be cancelled.

The next day at work was when Dave came up to me and told me what was going on. He said that the trumpet player had been complaining that he did not like my guitar playing and was threatening to leave the band unless they got rid of me and picked up a new guitar player. Since Dave was so gung-ho on having the horn section and not wanting to lose them, they apparently decided to go ahead and cut me. Without previously telling me their decision, they had already set up a new spot location to practice in and had already begun practicing with the new guitar player. Just like that and just that quick, I was out.

I had come to learn that's how things were done in Go-Go. In many cases, you are not told that you're cut from a band, you just find out. Naturally, I was disappointed and a bit hurt by the band's decision to have me cut, but what could I do? What was done was done, and it definitely wasn't the first time that I've been cut or kicked out of something. I survived. And if I didn't know anything else by this time in my life, I did know one thing; God does not close one door without opening an even better one for you. This much I understood. And, although I was very disappointed by how it all went down, I was also well with it.

THE UPSIDE DOWN PYRAMID PURSUIT

There was something that my Uncle Bernard (my cousin Byron's father) once said to me that I always remembered. I personally called it "The Upside Down Pyramid Pursuit." It goes something like this:

Let's say you start off your first time playing in a Go-Go band. In this Go-Go band there are 10 members, and out of the 10 members in the band, you're going to find maybe one who is really serious. Eventually that one member is going to move up to a higher level on the Pyramid Pursuit to another band that is a bit more serious than the current band.

Now in this next band that he/she is in, let's say there are again 10 members. And out of the 10 members, you are going to maybe find 3 who are extremely serious towards taking things even higher. And again, eventually those 3 members in that band are going to move up once again, whether together or separately, on the Pyramid Pursuit to a band on a higher level where there are more members that are more serious to take things even further.

Now we're on an even higher level of the Pyramid. And again, this band has 10 members, but in this particular band, there are 6 members who are extremely serious in pursuing it even stronger. This is the type of way that things are going to keep going until each member who is equally as serious to reaching the top of the Pyramid Pursuit as the others. This is the type of movement that has always happened with musicians/artists in Go-Go until all of a group of artists are on the same page.

TRYING TO GET HIRED BY RARE ESSENCE

Rare Essence was playing at the Metro Club, and apparently there were issues with the sound. James Funk's frustration towards the sound crew showed during the performance. When the band took an intermission break, Funk remained on the stage and made an announcement.

"Excuse me, everybody, but if there's a sound person in the house, make yourself known. We are looking for a new sound crew."

That was all I needed to hear. When Funk finally walked off the stage, I immediately approached him.

"Funk, I'm interested in working with the sound crew," I boasted.

He gave me a serious look. "Do you have any experience?"

I stood there confused as Funk went on.

"What is your educational background of school training in sound equipment engineering?"

I thought to myself, *Dag! I need to go to school to be a sound person?*

Funk's questions were enough to stop my pursuit for that moment, but the experience was also a sign that if I really was interested, I needed to find a school and take some classes. I went on a mission to be a soundman. I researched and found out that Omega recording studio, which was located in Rockville, Maryland, offered classes of applied recording arts and sciences in audio engineering, so I jumped on a metro bus and went there. However, I was not able to take the classes because I could not afford them. I eventually tossed that plan to the side and moved on.

1988

AND THE BEAT GOES ON

I would be lying if I say that I didn't get a bit depressed after being cut from Pure Elegance. In fact, it bothered me a whole lot. Up until that time, the only thing I knew that kept me happy other than being able to play my guitar was being able to play in a band. So there I was, just me and my guitar, but not with a band. My trust level also diminished a bit mainly because of how the situation with Pure Elegance took place. I felt blind-sided because I never saw it coming. I was cut from a band basically because a member either did not like my style of playing or did not like me personally.

But again, I still had my guitar and, either way you put it, I saw the whole thing as my cue telling me that I needed to get better and tighten up on my skills. The depression didn't stop me from wanting to tighten up my chops every chance I got, and every chance I got, that's what I did — worked on my homework. My guitar was like an extension to my arm. It had gotten to the point where if you saw me, most likely you also saw my guitar in my hand because I took it everywhere I went.

The major part of my life was the brand new experience in having a child. Circumstances took place that resulted in my infant daughter living with me. I was a young, single parent at the age of 23 that was trying to get on his feet and find a good job while pursuing my love of playing Go-Go. Since I was ripping and running at the time I was suddenly given custody, my Aunt June blessed me by allowing my daughter to stay with her. One great aspect of this arrangement was my Aunt June happened to live just a short walk away in Holly Park, Seat Pleasant. Therefore I would be at my Aunt June's house spending time with my daughter very often.

I actually ended up being at my aunt's house so much that sometimes my cousins Rob and Kelly were home, and we spontaneously would hang out together and hit a Go-Go. We would go see Little Benny and The Masters at the Metro Club on Wednesdays, Rare Essence at the Metro Club on Thursdays, and Rare Essence at the Black Hole on Saturdays. Actually, those were the only two bands that we were really interested in seeing at the time.

One day as I was walking through Holly Park to go over my aunt's house with my guitar in my hand, there was a guy standing in his front yard. "Hey, man! Do you play the guitar?" he called out and asked. Of course, it was obvious that apparently I must play since I was walking with the guitar case in my hand, but I went on and answered him anyway and walked over to him. I told him I did play the guitar. He introduced himself as Weaze and asked if I was playing with anyone at the time. I told him no, and he asked if I was interested in playing with a band he played with in the neighborhood called High Intensity. He played the trombone as well as percussion, so I thought to myself that it wouldn't hurt to check them out. Shortly after that I started going to the band practices with him, and I even did a few shows with them.

Eventually Weaze and I became pretty close. We played a short time with High Intensity, but this particular band was just a little too wild for me to be bothered with. If they weren't fighting each other all the time, they were getting into fights with others. When you get to a point where members in a band that you're playing with jump off the stage to engage in fights that are taking place in the crowd, it just may be time to reevaluate your current situation. I was not trying to be bothered with that, so I rolled out, and to my surprise, Weaze rolled with me.

Together we started playing with another band called Superior Groove. This particular band was actually located in uptown North West, DC right off of Georgia Avenue. Every week, Weaze and I would jump on the metro bus, guitar in my hand, trombone in his, and head to band practice on Rittenhouse Street.

One evening while Weaze and I were on the train, I noticed a nice looking, and jive phat, young lady sitting by herself, so I decided to pull up on her. I sat beside her and engaged her in conversation. Ten minutes later, and in the middle of my conversation with her, Weaze walked up, handed her a piece of paper, and said "Here. Call me."

Needless to say, I was pissed. I kind of understood the game, but I personally didn't play it nor did I enjoy people including me in it. Weaze crossing the line violated our friendship a little, but looking back, it was funny.

WHERE'S YOUR GUITAR?

One night after leaving band practice with Superior Groove, instead of going straight home, Weaze and I decided to go to the Metro Club to see Little Benny and The Masters play. I purchased a Mustang hooptie from my neighbor for only $200, so we were driving now. Since I had my guitar with me, I decided to put it in the trunk of my car so no one could see it and break my windshield trying to steal it while we were in the club.

As we went into the club, one of the first things I noticed was the guitarist Boolah Roper was not on stage with the band, but instead sitting in the table section in the club. I didn't think too much of it at the moment. I just assumed that he was taking himself a little break, so I grabbed a drink and headed to the front of the stage as I always did to watch the small details of the show. As the band was playing, I noticed that Benny called over to where Boolah was sitting and asked was he coming up on the stage to play. Boolah responded by motioning back with his hands in a gesture as if he was saying, "Pay me."

Benny looked towards me. "What's up, Shorty? Where's your guitar?"

I yelled, "It's outside in the car!"

Benny looked to Godfava and said, "He's got his guitar out in the car."

Nothing else was mentioned about my guitar after that, although I have to admit that had he asked me to go out to my car and get my guitar, I would have been ready to hit the stage. In fact, for the rest of that entire show, I was hoping that he would.

MASTERS WITH NO BENNY

One night while playing with Superior Groove at a spot out in Frederick, Maryland, I noticed 3 band names on the poster: Little Benny and The Masters, Pump Blenders, and us.

Although this was a spot that we frequently played with Pump Blenders, and it always had a decent sized crowd, on this particular night the place was packed. This was no doubt due to the fact that Little Benny and them were on the card.

Of course, we played first, delivering a 45 minute set of our material. Then Pump Blenders took the stage, giving the audience another 45 minutes of nonstop Go-Go music.

Finally, after a whole night of anticipation, along with the audience and Pump Blenders, we as a band stood in the crowd watching as Little Benny and The Masters took the stage. However, there was a problem. Although the majority of the band members were there, Benny, Godfava, and Elmo were not. Instead, they had a guest stand in as Lead Talker, and before beginning their set, they announced Benny was not going to be able to make it, then they stated they had a special guest who was going to hold the fort down for him.

This was a major disappointment. Although I loved the band as a whole, especially the material they played, Little Benny was no doubt the main attraction that made people come out to see them. He was the sole reason that the place was as packed as it was. The band still sounded nice. Although I was a bit disappointed in not being able to see Benny play, we still enjoyed ourselves.

PHONE CALL FROM LIL BENNY

The phone rang and my brother Chucky answered it. Seconds later, he extended it and told me that it was for me. I grabbed the phone and the voice on the other end said, "Hello, can I speak to Kevin?" The voice was familiar, but at that moment I still had no idea who it was.

"This is Kevin," I responded. "Who is this?"

"What's up, Kevin? This is Little Benny."

At first, I didn't even believe him. I thought it was somebody playing on my phone. First of all, how did he get my number? And more importantly, why would he be calling me? I found out later that he actually got in contact with my cousin Kelly, who lived in Holly Park with my Aunt June and my daughter, and got my phone number from him.

Benny went on to tell me that he was in the process of revamping his band. Apparently, the band was booking shows without his knowledge, and when they showed up to play, they would tell the crowd that Little Benny would not be able to make it. Benny went on to tell me all the details of how he found out about what they were doing. What instantly came to mind was what I just recently saw at the show we did with the "Little Benny-less" Masters and Pump Blenders. Although I didn't mention it to him on the phone, I knew exactly what he was talking about because I personally witnessed it. It all made sense to me then. With the exception of his band members Godfava and Elmo, he was replacing every position in the band.

He asked me if I would be available to come through their practice that night. Knowing that my car had just gotten temporarily impounded, I called my cousin Kelly and asked if he would run me over there to audition. The location where they were holding band practice was located in a basement of a house on the corner of 14th and Good Hope Road, South East. As Kelly and I entered the basement, Benny, Godfava, and Elmo were already there. Also present during this session was a drummer who went by the name of Shorty Dud, and a bass player named Vincent Tabbs. I recognized both from a band called AM/FM.

As I pulled my guitar out of the case and began plugging it into the amplifier, the first thing that Godfava asked me was who was my favorite guitar player in Go-Go. When I responded that my favorite guitar player was Whiteboy, the lead guitarist for Rare Essence and Godfava's former band member, he immediately jumped in my ass. It turns out his question was less of a question and more of a test because he began aggressively going in on me by telling me how my favorite guitar player should be Chuck Brown.

Maybe Godfava was right. After all, how could I debate with him? Godfava was part of the creation of the "One On One" — one of the most popular Go-Go grooves ever made, and many others. His name rang in the Go-Go community like that of a god. He earned the name "Godfather," but out of respect for Chuck Brown the Godfather of Go-Go, he spelled his name "Godfava." I'm sure Whiteboy learned plenty from Chuck, but Godfava didn't ask me who was the best guitar player, he asked who was my favorite. Another point to be made is I did not come up studying Chuck Brown's style of playing. I studied Whiteboy because Rare Essence was who I listened to the most when I practiced on my guitar. I was attracted to Whiteboy's style of playing because it was funkier than any of the other bands that I would listen to, and I wanted my style to be just as funky. I wanted to develop with the same type of process and precision that Whiteboy executed when playing songs on his guitar. I spent countless hours studying and practicing his style on songs such as "Working Up A Sweat," "What's That Fuss (Doin The Do)," and, of course, my all-time favorite, "Roll Call." Those were the type of songs that caught my attention as a guitar player because of the rugged and raw funkiness of them along with the hard scratching and strumming. That was how I developed my style in teaching myself how to play.

Although Godfava was probably right about how my inspiration should have been coming from Chuck, apparently that was not the case at that time. However, what his criticism did was open my eyes to listening to more of Chuck Brown's style of playing. No doubt it was much cleaner and precise than anyone else, but I loved what I loved. That raw, funky, hard-attacking strumming style that Whiteboy played is what appealed to me more than any other style.

As I began plugging up my guitar to the available amplifier, again Godfava came at me. This time he asked where my rig was. To be honest, I had no idea what he was talking about because I never heard of a rig regarding my guitar. These terms that he was hitting me with were new to me. Although I played in many bands in the neighborhoods, this was my very first time being within a camp on their level. This was a band that had already been making big noise in the city even before this particular camp started. They already put out records that were hits in the city. They already played in arenas such as the Capital Center several times. Up until this point, I had never been anywhere even close to where they reached at that point. Godfava's drilling me alone had me thinking that I already failed the audition before I even struck a note on my guitar. Saying that the drilling and criticizing was rather intimidating to me would be an understatement, but I also recognized that getting into the camp would open a whole new world of knowledge and experience for me.

Since I was already familiar with Little Benny and The Masters' material thanks to PA tapes, the performance part of the audition really was not bad. My already knowing the material is actually what saved me. Whatever song Benny called, I was able to jump right into it and go with the flow seamlessly. Apparently it was good enough because by the end of the night I was officially a new member of the band Little Benny and The Masters.

The next morning as Weaze and I headed out for another day of work, I was excited to tell him exactly what happened the night before. I began explaining to him the call I received from Benny and then later auditioning and making it into the band. At that moment, Weaze was suddenly more excited about the situation than I was. He immediately stopped, leaped in the air, and started yelling, "I'm gonna be a Master! I'm gonna be a Master!"

His excitement about the Little Benny and The Masters thing actually lessened mine. At that very moment I felt his excitement must have been stemming from the assumption that because I was now in the band, that meant he would instantly be a member of the band as well by association alone. The biggest thing that I did not want was to be under the pressure of trying to help get him into a band that I barely got in.

Weaze was no doubt a very motivated person with strong desires and drive, but based on his level of playing at the time, he was not ready to perform on the level that Little Benny required. And considering the drilling that I had just gone through with Godfava, I didn't think that I was in a strong enough position to bring another person in nor did I want to jeopardize my position by trying to do so. Once I solidified my position in Little Benny and The Masters, and if I caught wind that Benny was looking to add someone to the horn section or was open to the idea of adding someone in an area that Weaze could fit into, I would definitely have suggested Benny allow him to audition.

I immediately informed Weaze of all of that, and that was fine with him. Weaze was the type of cat that didn't need a hand to guide him anywhere for the most part. All you had to do was just open up the door, and he'd get it himself. The fact that we were close meant that he would be available to the inside and try to convince the band himself to let him audition, which he unsuccessfully ended up trying to do many times.

PLAYING AT THE CAPITAL CENTER

Finally, at the completion of the full revamping of Little Benny and The Masters, the members were Benny on trumpet and lead rap, Godfava and Markie Owens on keyboards, Elmo on congas, CJ Jones (formally of Redds and The Boys and CJ's Uptown Crew) on saxophone, Shorty Dud on drums, Vincent Tabbs on bass guitar, David Green (formally of Rare Essence) on the roto-tom, and me on lead guitar. Eventually, Vincent left the group, as well as Shorty Dud (who went to play with Rare Essence). Gary Smith came in as the new bass player, and Lil Mike on the drums.

In 1987, the Go-Go community had been celebrating and rallying around a video that had been released of a show that was entitled *Go-Go Live at The Capital Center*. Go-Go bands performing at the Capital Center were not anything new. Many bands played at Back To School Boogie type of events with Hip-Hop and national R&B acts, but *Go-Go Live at The Capital Center* was the very first time that a show had taken place at this venue that consisted of nothing but Go-Go bands. Before then, the only venues that hosted such large Go-Go events of this magnitude were places such as the Washington Coliseum and RFK Stadium (where the Washington Redskins played). Having such an event of that magnitude at the Capital Center actually placed a new type of significance towards Go-Go music. This was considered the national stage to play on.

The bands that performed on that card were Chuck Brown and The Soul Searchers, Rare Essence, Experience Unlimited, Little Benny and The Masters, Hot Cold Sweat, Junkyard Band, and Go-Go Lorenzo, to include a special performance by DC Scorpio, who performed during Chuck Brown's set.

By the time 1988 rolled around, and with the success of the *Go-Go Live* at the Capital Center event, G Street Express was already gearing up and preparing for a second event, *Go-Go Live II at the Capital*

Center. Of course, since I was now a member of Little Benny and The Masters, this brought extreme excitement to me. It immediately took me back to the days when I used to go see bands playing there, and now there I was getting ready to perform there myself.

The bands that were selected this go around were Chuck Brown and The Soul Searchers, Rare Essence (who had been making noise in the streets with songs such as "Lock It," as well as a rapper who went by the name of Stinky Dink), Experience Unlimited (who had just come back home from a tour promoting their national hit single "Da Butt"), Little Benny and The Masters, Junkyard Band (who were super hot in the streets with the song "Hee-Haw"), Pleasure (the all-female Go-Go Band) and DJ Kool (who had been making noise with a hot single called "The Music Ain't Loud Enough").

This also served as the moment and opportunity for Little Benny himself to solidify to a large audience at one time that he indeed had not fallen off. Due to the fact that he ended up having to revamp his entire band, one of his main goals was to rebuild and strengthen the band's street ranking. So in essence, our particular performance for the event we themed the "Guess Who's Back" performance of the show. Just like he solidified his position in the ranks during the first *Go-Go Live*, especially with his hit song "Cat in the Hat," the mentality was that this go around we would have to do the same thing. We were reintroducing ourselves to the Go-Go community, while competing with the heavyweights on the same show. This meant that every aspect of our performance of this show would have to be not only 100% on par, but just as equal to the energy that was given at the first show, if not even better. The songs that Benny selected for us to play were "I'm King," "Ladies of the Eighties," and "Mercedes," all of which were released just prior to my joining the band.

For the attire we were going to where, Benny brought in a tailor, and we were all measured and fitted for custom-made, all-white, Polo jumpsuits. Benny's particular jumpsuit also included a long, white coat that displayed a large Polo symbol on the back.

For choreography, we went right back to the same place where Benny had gone to have his set choreographed in the first Go-Go Live event, which were The Bren-Carr Dancers. We worked on steps choreographed by them that would be designated to each song that was listed for us to play. Needless to say, by the night of this event, we were more than ready.

Some of us arrived through the stage entrance at the Capital Center early on the day of the event and just relaxed in our designated dressing room until the rest of the band arrived. The entire time I was not just relaxing, I was also smelling the roses and pinching myself at the reality that there I was about to play in what we considered the most significant venue in the region. When I was growing up, this was the place that I had come to for countless concerts, Bullets basketball games, and even the Ice Capades, not to mention that it was also the main venue for high school graduation ceremonies.

Playing on the top of a Slick Rick song entitled "Hey Young World," we opened up our set vamping the beat, choreographically stepping onto the stage while chanting over and over again, "Guess Who's Back!" By the end of the night, we successfully accomplished what we set out to do — inform the crowd that, yes, indeed Little Benny and The Masters were back!

Although this particular show was not released on video as the first one had been, segments of it did make it on a popular cable music video channel called The Box. Our performance of the song "I'm King" was the segment of our set that was showcased on it.

ROBBED AT GUNPOINT

Weeks after playing the Capital Center, and on the eve of Halloween, Weaze and I were walking through my neighborhood heading to my parents' house. Suddenly a car had rolled up on us. Weaze immediately peeped what was going on, yelled, "Jump Out!" and took off running. By the time I realized what was happening, two guys had already jumped out of the car and brandished a silver-plated .38 in my face. Both were wearing Pittsburgh Steelers hooded Starter jackets and white hockey masks like Jason. I thought my life was about to be over.

With the gun pointed directly in my face, they yelled for me to take my leather coat off. Not wanting to give them any reason to pull that trigger, I did what they ordered and began pulling off my leather coat. As the one with the gun grabbed for it, the other guy circled around me and then punched me in my jaw. The punch did not faze me, but it gave me the realization that apparently these were some young cats. I decided that I was going to give them the impression that the punch did indeed faze me, so I decided to flip myself over the wooden fence that was behind me as if he was Mike Tyson. My thought process was that if I made this guy think he knocked me out, then just maybe they would be satisfied with that and would not shoot me. And just as I had hoped, when I flipped myself over the fence and laid still on the ground, they quickly jumped in their car and pulled off. I then waited in that position for several seconds longer just to ensure they were gone. Then I got up and ran.

By the time I reached the building where my parents lived, Weaze and my father were running up the street towards me. Weaze explained that when he looked back and saw me falling to the ground, he thought they shot me, so he ran and got my father. They were coming back up the street to handle the situation.

There was no question that I was thankful to God for being with me during that moment. Although I was a little shaken up and jive upset at having my leather coat taken from me, I was also aware that it could have been my life taken instead of my coat. I have no idea where or how I came up with the idea so quickly of making them think that they knocked me out, but I was definitely thankful to God that it worked.

After the dust settled, I began thinking and then became angry. I blurted out, "Dag! They got my tape!" I didn't give a damn about my leather coat, but inside of it was a PA tape of a show we did down in North Carolina just a few days prior. I was upset about being robbed and assaulted, but I was more upset about losing that tape because it was the only one of its kind.

A MASTER NO MORE

As I was sitting home one night practicing on my guitar, I received a call from a member from another band who had been practicing at the same new location that we just started using for rehearsals. He was telling me that his band was in the process of looking for a new lead guitar player, and he wanted to know if I was interested in playing with them.

One thing about me is that I have always been the type of person to be loyal to a team that I'm with, and I was never interested in ever doing side jobs outside of my camp. Although I appreciated the invite, I reminded him that I was currently playing with Benny. That was when he hit me with the news that literally made my heart drop.

He told me that he was at Vince's studio the night before and noticed that Little Benny and The Masters were practicing there with a different guitar player, and that he assumed that I was no longer in the band. I had no idea how to respond to him because I had no idea what he was talking about. I wasn't even sure at the time that I could take his word for it. As far as I was concerned, he could have been just telling me that to make me get upset, leave my band, and go ahead and join his band. I had to hear this from the mouth of Benny himself, so that's exactly what I sought out to do.

Immediately after hanging up the phone with him, I jumped in my car and drove to Benny's house. I knocked on the door, and when he opened it, without stepping into the house, I simply asked if it were true that they got another guitar player. Benny said it was true, and he went on to tell me that it wasn't working out with me on the guitar, so they were trying out some other options. Although I was no doubt disappointed, what more could I do but to accept it?

1989-
1992

THE WOODSHED

After running around for a minute with a bit of free time on my hands, I had gotten the word that Little Benny and The Masters were scheduled to play at a venue called the All Around Race Way. Since that spot was in my area, I decided that I was going to go ahead and check them out.

One of the very first things I noticed when entering the place and looking up on the stage was that there was no guitar player up there playing with them. Another thing that I noticed was with the exception of Godfava, all of the members on the stage were new, some were actually previous members. I mean, it had only been approximately 2 months since I was fired from the group, and this was the very first time I had seen them since then.

When the band finally finished their set, I went up on the stage to holla at Benny right quick. Anybody in their right mind already knew what I wanted to holla at him about. I asked him where was his guitar player, and he told me that it didn't work out with him. He then asked if I was interested in coming back in the band. In truth, he didn't even have to ask me that. Getting my position back was the main reason I approached him about it in the first place, but the fact that he did ask made me feel all the more welcomed in doing so.

He went on to tell me to bring my guitar and come to the practice the following week. He also let me know that they were no longer practicing at the previous location, but instead now practicing at his cousin's house, which was located in Capitol Heights, Maryland. This was perfect for me because the new spot was actually right down the street from where I lived.

The following week I did exactly as he said. In fact, I showed up early because I wanted them to know just how serious I was about coming back into the band. When I arrived at the new location of the practice spot, I was greeted by his cousin Keith Holmes. Keith was a much older guy than the rest of us, and his knowledge of music made him a very strong mentoring source for us. He was a musician, but he was looked upon and considered more of an OG musician because he had come up in the music scene during the pre-Go-Go error of live bands, playing with the popular local bands such as The Matadors and Nation's Time. In essence, he was very well equipped with the knowledge of the ins and outs of the local band scene, and in truth, he became a valuable asset to the musical direction of the band. I introduced myself to him as a former lead guitar player in the band, but he already knew who I was, and was expecting me at rehearsal that night.

Eventually the members of the band began entering rehearsal. Elmo was recently put in jail, so instead of him on congas, there was a new percussionist who went by the name of Nathanial "Bouncey" Lucas. I was very familiar with Bouncey due to the fact that he used to play with a band called High Potential, which was a band we frequently played on the same card with during the time that I was playing with Superior Groove.

Instead of Lil Mike on the drums, Kiggo Wellman was now the drummer, and he happened to be the previous member of the band. He was also the cousin of top rated Go-Go drummer Ricky "Sugar Foot" Wellman of Experience Unlimited and Chuck Brown and The Soul Searchers. Former vocalist Bryant "Luther" Roberts was also back in the band. On the keyboards was a new member who went by the name of Deandre "Dee" Minor, and on the bass guitar was a new member named Michael Baker. Also now in the band were former original members of Rare Essence John "Big Horn" Jones on the trombone, Rory "DC" Felton on the saxophone, Scotty Haskel on keyboard, and Tyrone "Jungle Boogie" Williams on the congas.

Eventually Kiggo again left the group and was replaced by Alonzo Robinson, a former member of Trouble Funk. Luther also left the group again and was replaced by former Rare Essence and Little Benny and The Masters member Michael Muse. Also, Godfava eventually returned to the band as well. Former Experience Unlimited and Masters trombonist Mike "Hard-Step" Taylor had also come back to the camp. Occasionally, drummer William "JuJu" House, percussionist Milton "GoGo Mickey" Freeman, and former Masters member Terry Lambert, who would rotate on both the drums and the bass, would sit in with us.

As a matter of fact, the band began to be filled with so many original and former Rare Essence members that it began to feel like playing with the original Rare Essence. Because of this, it had gotten to the point where people were requesting to hear us play many of the original Rare Essence songs that these members were known to be an intricate part of. Of course, this was fine with me because I loved being able to have the opportunity to play that stuff.

Eventually I began spending more and more time at Keith's outside of the practice sessions with Little Benny and The Masters because Keith schooled me to many aspects of music. I had a hunger to learn more, and he was nice enough to take me under his wing and educate me on the ins and outs of music as well as the music business. His practice spot began to serve as a practice spot for many of the other bands in the area. Bands such as EU, Chuck Brown and The Soul Searchers, Young Groovers, and many others had a home there, and my being there all the time turned into my opportunity to be able to run the sound for these bands while they were practicing. This added towards my knowledge of being able to know how to run the sound for bands.

It had become such a popular practice spot that Keith eventually gave it the name The Woodshed — a place for musicians to come and shed and strenuously work out on their craft. There was a saying that he used to always recite which was, "When you come into this woodshed to work out, there should be chips of wood dust on your shoulders that need to be brushed off when you leave. If there is no dust on your shoulders, that means your workout wasn't up to par to where it should be." And speaking of nicknames, Keith is the person that began calling me "Kato" instead of "Kevin."

Chuck Brown would come through sometimes just to say hello. He would usually have his two very young sons with him. During our breaks, he would sit down and shoot the breeze with us for a little while. He was the supreme teacher, and he enjoyed answering all the questions we students asked. He also shared stories of DC music history with us.

One thing I noticed was everybody referred to him as "Pops." I personally would not refer to him by that title because I always felt it was a term of endearment that only members of his band and those very close to him had the right to use. Later, of course, I realized that it indeed was okay for me to refer to him as that as well. Not only was it a term of endearment, it was a term of honor and respect.

MICROPHONE CHECK

One thing I did have an immediate understanding of in coming back into the band was the fact that I was going to try to have to figure out a way to stamp my position in the band some kind of way. I realized that when I got into the band the first time, one of the biggest tasks was to pick up where Benny's former band members left off. Musically, they were tight and on point. Boolah Roper was the guitar player before me, and without a doubt in my mind one of the baddest lead guitar players in the city. I knew that filling his shoes was a level I had not quite reached yet skill wise, so my plan was to bring in something totally different as far as style and technique was concerned.

The most exciting thing about my years of playing in Go-Go bands is the energy that's generated mainly due to the crowds who are directly in front of your face just a few feet away. Their participation and involvement towards the success of Go-Go is so eminent that indirectly they are actually co-creators of many songs that are created by the bands.

After every performance, no matter how tired I may have been, I would get an ultra burst of adrenaline and just wired with emotions, thoughts, and vibrations. The love you get from sharing songs, our songs as well as songs that inspired us...Oooh, boy! There's just nothing like it! It's intimate, raw, strong, unifying, and so special. Aaaaaaaah, music is so powerful! The more I was finding myself on the front line, the more I was discovering this.

Slowly but surely I was given significant speaking roles on the microphone, which would, of course, require me to have to be on the front line. This began when we started playing a cover song by the rap group 3rd Bass called "Pop Goes the Weasel." When we performed this song, the rap verses were divided among Benny, DC, and me. The reason they took a chance on me joining in on rapping the song was because while doing my homework of learning the song on my guitar, I had also written down the lyrics to the entire song. When I presented my guitar part in the next practice, I was so deep in the groove and into the moment that I began rapping the lyrics while I was playing a part of it. Benny was surprised. He said, "Man, I didn't know you could rap."

Benny was so impressed that he allowed me to have that part of the song, which turned out to be one of the popular selections that we were playing at the time. It had even gotten to the point where some of the ladies in the crowd started calling me "Pop" because the song chorus was "Pop Goes The Weazel." Before then, they were all just saying, "Who's the little guy on the guitar?"

After that, just about the majority of all the cover songs we played that contained rap verses were split between either Benny, DC, and me or I would just do the entire song.

With me leading, we played covers such as Naughty By Nature's "Everything's Gonna Be Alright," EPMD's "Crossover," which both Benny and I shared the versus, and Black Sheep's "The Choice Is Yours." I was also selected to be part of the background singing whenever we would play R&B covers, supporting the lead vocalist which was either Michael Muse or Jungle Boogie.

Finally, there was one song that was so unique in the flow, delivery, and pronunciations that they decided to give it entirely to me. This was a cover by two Hip-Hop artists named Drayz and Skoob. They called themselves Das Efx, and the name of the song was "They Want Efx." It was a style created by them that combined nonsensical verses with a fast-paced flow that included words that ended with "iggedy."

This rap style was actually nothing new to the DC area because there was a local rapper at the time who went by the name of Stinky Dink that delivered this same exact style whenever stepping on the stage to perform with Rare Essence. The difference between Das Efx's style and Stinky Dink's was Drayz and Skoob shifted their verses back and forth towards each other, and their lyrics consisted of infinite pop culture references. Whereas Stinky Dink, who was commonly known as "The Rickety Raw One," basically referenced himself.

Since I was the only one in the band who was going to perform the Das Efx song, I had to cover both Drayz and Skoob's parts. This actually turned out to be a bit of a challenge. If you were not taking enough air into your diaphragm and breathing correctly while delivering the versus, you could easily run out of breath before getting to the end of any particular measure. However, I practiced and did so well at shows and pleased the crowds that Benny decided to give me another Das Efx song called "Mic Checka."

Before long I was practically given all of the hip-hop songs that we covered. This actually began solidifying my stamp in the band and securing my position. In all honesty, rapping actually began taking precedence over my guitar playing because if I didn't know anything else, delivering dynamic stage presence and performances were what I knew all too well. This, of course, was based on my theater and stage experience. The one thing that I definitely was not afraid of was the microphone.

This eventually ignited a spark in me that generated a growing interest in rapping. I began to focus on it so much that I began writing songs, and even going as far as setting up a home studio where I would write rap lyrics and create the music to accompany them. I would then record them making my own demos. With money that I received from my tax return refund, I decided to go all out. I went out to Rockville to Chuck Levin's Music and bought a TASCAM Porta

One 4 -Track Recorder, an Alesis HR-16 Drum Machine, and a Korg M1 Keyboard Workstation. And along with my Fender Stratocaster Guitar, I setup the mini studio in the living room of my apartment. Of course, my girlfriend Pam was not happy about that one bit.

Taking the advice that I was given by my cousin Byron of Rare Essence, I connected the HR-16 Drum Machine to the Korg M1 Keyboard Workstation through the midi connection for the purpose of having the two devices stay in sync for the length of a song. My little brother Chucky and I wrote and recorded tons of songs for the next few years for our own individual projects as well as for other people. The only thing that I ever did besides playing with the band and going to work was stay up in my mini-studio writing and recording; this was something else that Pam was not very happy about. Not only did Chucky and I record tracks there, sometimes my fellow band members Scotty Haskel, Michael Muse, and DC would come over and lay some tracks as well.

While working on my own music projects at home, I even came up with a little, catchy name for myself based on my surroundings. Since I was already known by the name Kato within the Go-Go community, I tagged a title at the end of it, which would be my rap name — Kato The Inner-City Groover. Of course, the "inner-city groover" part was adapted from Rare Essence because they were widely known as the "Inner-City Groovers." Since I figured the style of music I played was inspired by their music, I felt the title to be appropriate.

I never talked about that to anyone outside of my home studio though. However, I did use that name when I entered one of my songs in Songwriter's Association of Washington's Mid-Atlantic Songwriting Competition (I actually received an award for writing that song). Beyond that, I never really took things any further with my songs other than basically playing them around the house. All of my performing of any type of raps were done on the stage when performing with Little Benny and The Masters. And whenever I wanted to have live percussions in my tracks, I would take my equipment over to The Woodshed, and Bouncey would record the live conga and roto-tom tracks for me.

Chucky was already deep into writing lyrics. He had a notebook full of raps that he had written, and he already came up with a stage name for himself — Cash M N Chuck. The majority of the times when I would be out playing with the band, Chucky would always come with me because we both shared that same passion for music, and especially Go-Go. He had no interest in trying to join any of the bands I was in. When working on projects with him, I wore the producer hat and not the artist had. I never rapped in Chucky's songs at all. He did all the writing and rapping of his own songs, and I only participated in the laying of the music around his rapping.

The one thing that I really was impressed with about Chucky's style was just how deep he was with his lyrics and the wide range of subject matter that he talked about. He would come to me reciting some new lyrics that he had just written, and as he rapped them to me, I would begin to develop a sound in my head as far as what type of beats, keyboard carpets, and rhythm should go around the lyrics he delivered. The object was to not take away or upstage his lyrics, but instead to simply add flavor to what he already created lyrically. We would spend hours at a time in sessions.

Eventually times got rough as they sometimes do, and I ended up pawning the drum machine and 4-track recorder, and selling my Korg M1 Keyboard to Mike Hughes of the AM/FM band; something else that my girlfriend Pam was not too happy about.

GIRLS

One of the perks of playing in a popular Go-Go band, or any Go-Go band for that matter, is the attention received from women. For a single guy, this was a blessing that one would take with stride and enjoy the perks available. Now for a guy that was in a relationship, this would sometimes lead to nothing but trouble…trouble…trouble. I was a guy that fell into the latter category.

I was not just in a relationship, I was in a relationship with a woman who was not a big fan of Go-Go. In other words, she liked it just the same as she liked any other general musical entertainment. Therefore, she wasn't into the music, she wasn't into the culture, and she didn't attend a go-go unless there was some type of special occasion going on and she had to come to support me. Personally, I preferred it that way. I've been playing long enough to know not to bring your girl around the Go-Go scene nor was I interested in any girls who I'd see at every single go-go that I would go to or perform. I always wanted to make sure that my personal relationships remained personal, private, and separate from Go-Go, which I considered my job.

Pam and I had known each other since we were little kids, but we didn't start talking to each other until I came home from the Army. During the time that I was playing with Superior Groove and sitting in with other bands was when we started hooking up. Eventually we moved into an apartment together, and it was shortly after that I started playing with Benny for the second time.

I did not want to have to worry about things such as other guys trying to hit on her. More than that, I didn't want other girls being jealous of her and trying to make things difficult for her by trying to fight her or anything stupid like that. When I was home, that's where I wanted to be. I wanted to leave the Go-Go where the Go-Go was, and have my home be what a home should be. I looked forward to little things like coming home after a show at night and walking in the bedroom seeing her asleep or simply just sitting up waiting for me. In that kind of situation, trust played a big part on both sides.

Up until I started playing with Little Benny, a band member crossing the line was sometimes an issue with other bands that I would play or sit in with. It was always a thing of some band member secretly trying to talk to or hit on her behind my back. Sometimes they would call the house when they knew I was at practice or a show, or even come by our apartment with lines like, "I was just stopping through to check up on you because since you're Kato's girl, that makes you like my little sister." They'd do little dumb, slick shit like that, never realizing she would tell me. That was the type of environment that I did not want us to be part of. I wanted us to be separated from that silliness.

Little Benny and The Masters was the first band I played with where I felt a sense of family environment. It actually became an environment that I felt very comfortable in bringing Pam into because of the location where we practiced, which was at Benny's cousin Keith's house a.k.a. The Woodshed. They made it a big deal, whether intentionally or not, to make everyone feel at home there. For example, as the members of the band would show up for practice, it was not uncommon that we would sometimes bring our girlfriends, fiancées, or wives with us. As we would head downstairs to begin practicing, our women would all remain upstairs, gathered in their women circle talking, watching movies, etc. That kind of atmosphere made it comfortable for me to bring Pam into it. It allowed her to see exactly how the band functioned, and it also helped to keep her in the know and involved directly in what I was doing without her having to be in the club.

Unfortunately, there are still serpents that can infiltrate their way into a relationship, which is actually something that I did not take into consideration. Thinking that our keeping our relationship out of the go-go would be a thing that would protect our relationship kind of played against us. Though she did not come to go-gos, that didn't mean that she didn't know people who knew people that did. That can sometimes play a part as far as the rumor mill goes because people who knew about our relationship would sometimes feed false negativity to her.

I remember a situation where word had gotten to her that after a show we did at the Metro Club, I took some girl and her friends out to breakfast and then had sex with the girl. Of course, this was not true. I didn't even know the girl they were talking about, but when people feed that kind of negativity to a person, it starts to plant seeds of doubt and develop thoughts of the possibility that something like that could actually happen.

First of all, I was not making the kind of money to impress some girl and her friends by taking them out to eat. I was never the perpetrating, big Willie type of cat. Not only that, but for me to mess up what I had at home with people who kind of spend their lives at the clubs and go-go was not a route that I wanted to take. I always carried a family mentality, and family was something that I always wanted to have. I never wanted to jeopardize that, especially with any type of woman who could be with me one week and some other Go-Go band member the next. These would be the same women that you would see just about every place you went when it came to Go-Go. I'm not knocking their groove, but that was their life, but not one I wanted to have. That's what they did.

I'm not going to lie. Many women that came out to our shows were attractive...very attractive. Some of them were phat as a mug. However, the thought of losing what I had at home to an individual that I knew I couldn't trust as far as I could throw a rock was not a world that I was interested in living in. I loved playing music in the band, and the women that came with that environment were not the reason I loved playing music. Sure there were times without a doubt when I could have hooked up with a woman after a show and kicked it over her house or some motel, but the risk of losing what I had at home was something I was not willing to take. And when those type of rumors did infiltrate our relationship, these were the things I found myself having to consistently remind her of.

Eventually the rumors and stories became too heavy and Pam and I broke up, but definitely not by choice. Looking back though, there is no doubt that I was blind to see exactly what she was going through and having to deal with. Not to mention what some of her friends and family could've also been feeding towards it.

There were definitely other things that played into straining our relationship. One was the fact that I had gotten so headstrong into doing this whole music thing for a career that I put regular employment on the backseat. My focus was strictly on the music kind of like the way I messed things up during my Duke Ellington years. My focus was strictly on pursuing a career in music whereas her focus pointed towards working a regular full-time job with full benefits and opportunities for advancement, and years of growth towards one day retiring from that same job. My focus was on getting a job to maintain little things while focusing my biggest energy towards the music. That's a very difficult philosophy to place on someone who depends on you.

That relationship was when I learned that you both have to come from the same place, with the same ideals, and the same goals, with the same type of dreams, and the same desires. I never understood why she didn't see mine, and she never understood why I couldn't see hers. There is no question that I loved her with all my heart, body, and soul, but I just did not know how to fully express it the way she needed, while at the same time trying to pursue the music thing. I did not know how to be about both at the same time. Although that played a heavy role in our demise, the rumors were what brought us down.

LITTLE BENNY
and THE MASTERS ON THE MOVE

In addition to performing at clubs, Benny took the initiative to give back to the community. Little Benny and The Masters performed at charity events for the homeless, fundraisers, WPGC's Adopt-A-Block functions held throughout the city, and block parties. Benny even had us play directly in front of his house for the kids and everyone else in his neighborhood. All of this was done for free and out of the kindness of Benny's heart.

We even performed at Marion Barry's celebration party when he won the mayoral seat after being incarcerated. Northeast Groovers also performed at the event. We had the mayor, his political constituents, and his supporters partying!

Marion Barry often showed up at many of our outside neighborhood community events. He enjoyed the music and the people of the community. It was normal to see him stop by and show support for the love and positivity going on. It was also normal for a whole bunch of kids to gather around him as he walked through. They'd hug him, shake his hand, take pictures with him, and talk to him. He loved it.

A very interesting not-for-profit move that Benny made was partnering with Breeze, the owner of the Metro Club. Together, they threw kiddie cabaret shows for little children at the Metro Club. Benny and Breeze organized a team to decorate, have games, and prepare and serve food for kids, Little Benny and The Masters performed. Parents brought their dressed-up kids to the kiddie cabarets, and the admission only covered the costs of food and prizes. We did it for the kids of the community.

One of the most interesting places we performed was at Lorton Correctional Facility, the largest jail in the area. It's located in Virginia, and we'd stroll in there and put on a show for the inmates and visiting family and friends. What's interesting about playing there is that Elmo, former conga player for our group, was an inmate at Lorton, and whenever we played there, the warden actually allowed him to get on stage and perform with us.

Elmo wasn't their average inmate. Not only was he a musician, he was extremely popular with Little Benny and The Masters to the point where Benny titled a song on his first album after him — "Elmo Get Busy." Bouncey was so cool that he stepped aside for a little while at these shows and let Elmo perform with us. The inmates yelled, "Elmo get busy one time!" as Elmo hit the stage and went to work on Bouncey's congas. Most of the guards were part of Go-Go culture and fans of Little Benny and The Masters, so they wanted to see Elmo perform with The Masters again. On a side note, outside of our shows at Lorton, Elmo never played with Little Benny and The Masters again.

Little do people know that when it comes to creating Go-Go songs, inspiration can come from anywhere. During one of our performances at Lorton, while we were in the middle of a strong pocket, a large group of gay and transgender inmates, who were dancing together in the middle of the crowd, made their way to the front of the stage. They were dancing hard, and all of them were feminine; some were dressed as women. Suddenly, Benny started chanting, "Uh-oh! Uh-oh! Here comes the bammas!" over and over again. This was a chant coming from an MC Hammer song called "Here Comes The Hammer," but Benny changed the word "Hammer" to "Bammas" in referencing the party crowd that came to the front of the stage. They even began dancing harder, smiling, and nodding as if to say, "Yes! We have an official title. We are the bammas of Lorton."

Following Benny's lead, we began to vamp in our Go-Go rendition to accompany the chant. We ended up having so much fun vamping the song at that particular show that we added the song to our playlist when performing at other shows. We even recorded and released it on our album called "Take Me Out To The Go-Go." If that particular group didn't make their way to the stage at Lorton, we would've never played the song.

WOL

Although Go-Go music was without a doubt the most popular music on the streets, and bands were producing studio recorded albums in addition to the PA tapes that were being released in the streets, very rarely did Go-Go ever get any radio play — especially FM radio. As a matter fact, it almost never did with the exception of maybe a song or two on Howard University's station WHUR. Of course, Chuck Brown's music did not always fit into this category, especially with his bigger hits such as "Bustin' Loose" and "Back It On Up (Sho' Ya Right)." But finally there was one radio station that started playing Go-Go music in regular rotation. This was an AM radio station called WOL.

Every weekday evening, WOL broadcasted an all Go-Go radio show that was hosted by a radio jock by the name of Big Brother Konan. From 7pm until 11pm every evening, he would play nothing but Go-Go records. Songs from groups such as Hot Cold Sweat, Experience Unlimited, Rare Essence, Trouble Funk, Junkyard Band, Little Benny and The Masters, Petworth, Plump Blenders, Redds and The Boys, and just about every other band that were releasing studio productions were finally filling the airwaves in the city. It had gotten so popular with the youth that it began to show serious competition with WHUR's *Quiet Storm* program, which was at the time the most popular. This was solely due to the show's focusing strictly on Go-Go.

WOL was a popular station in the DC area years prior with the older generation who were tuned in to on-air personalities such as Petey Greene, Moon Man Bakos, and The Big Poppa. Now with Big Brother Konan in the evening driver's seat, it allowed the station to generate a whole new generation of devoted listeners, which in turn gave Go-Go a stronger significance within the city. They gave us the ability of feeling that we actually did have staying power, but that was only until the station owner Kathy Hughes eventually decided that she was going to pull the plug on the Go-Go show. She removed it entirely from the WOL airwaves.

When word got around that Konan's show would indeed be pulled from the airwaves, many people and bands in the Go-Go community gathered together to form a committee. The purpose for this committee was to develop a peaceful plan of protest with hopes of successfully encouraging WOL to change their minds. The object was to show them just how significant and important this music was to the generation, community, and culture. It was also demonstrating just how impactful it was to the individual musicians, especially the kids who were playing in these bands.

On the rainy morning of Monday, February 18, 1991, people from the different bands, as well as the fans, all gathered at Hechinger Mall parking lot on Benning Road where the protest march was set to begin. Together we all walked down H Street, North East and stopped on the corner of 4th and H Street, North East — the front door of the WOL radio station.

As successful as the plan and march had been, the efforts basically resulted in no success. We all gathered in front of the window of the WOL radio station asking for Ms. Kathy Hughes to come out and address us, but she never came out. Instead, a representative came out and basically told us how much he respected what we were doing and trying to accomplish, however the radio show would still be removed from the station. And just as he stated, Big Brother Konan's Go-Go radio show on WOL was no more.

STUDIO

Up until this point of playing with Little Benny and The Masters, I still had not gotten the opportunity to be able to participate in a studio recording with them. The last studio recordings released by them were actually recorded before I started playing with them, despite the fact they were released while I was in the band. And those songs were, "Uptown Ain't Kicking It," "Ladies of the 80s," "Mercedes," and "I'm King," the same songs that I had been given to learn when I first joined. The regular PA tapes of our live shows being released in the streets were cool, but I wanted to be on a studio record.

We began the process of putting a new project together. Although it would be released as a studio recording, it was actually a live recording session that took place at the Metro Club, and then taken to the studio to clean up. It was going to be produced by EU's drummer "JuJu" House. There were also special guests who took the stage and joined in some of the songs with us. In fact, the recording ended up being more like a jam session rather than the structured format that we practiced. The different guests who joined the stage with us were Byron Jackson and GoGo Mickey from Rare Essence, and Tino Jackson and JuJu himself from EU. The album was titled *Little Benny - Getting Funky Up In Here.*

Unfortunately, that release did not do quite well in the streets as everyone expected or hoped it would do. In truth, the type of material we played on this recording was the type of material that started us getting criticized in the streets for being too musical, i.e., playing too much music. We played songs such as "Killer Joe," "Walk," and a Thelonious Monk tune called "Round Midnight."

Benny decided to go back into the studio and release another one, but strictly studio this time. With so many former original Rare

Essence members now in the band, it was already quite a crowd pleaser to hear us play some of old songs that they were originally part of creating, so we had to incorporate that feature. We were not going to do this like the last project. It was going to be a straight studio recording in a live format, which means we would play it the same way that we would play on the stage. In other words, we would not stop in between songs, and we would not just lay individual tracks. Instead, we would play them as a whole band together at the same time.

The title of this album was *Take Me Out To The Go-Go*, and we did the recording at Black Pond Studio, which was owned and engineered by a cat named Chris Biondo. Black Pond Studio was large enough to allow the ability to record in the live format that we wanted, while at the same time giving us the ability to separate the instruments so that they wouldn't bleed on each other's tracks. For example, the drums were setup alone in one room, the congas were set in a separate room, and the guitars and keyboards could be in any room because those instruments plugged directly into the board. The people who were going to be laying the vocals on tracks, i.e. Benny, Mike Muse and Jungle Boogie, were also in another room. Therefore without being able to see each other the way we can on stage, we had to rely solely on listening for the cues through our headphones. Benny would call the cues through his mic, and we would execute as called.

The old Rare Essence hits that we recorded were "What's That Fuss," "Do It On Down," "Roll Call," and "One On One." We also recorded some of the newer stuff that we were playing at the time to include "Jungle Boogie Fever," "Living Color," and "Here Comes The Bamas." This album release did well in the streets. As far as I was concerned, it solidified a mark on my resume that I finally participated in a studio release of a Go-Go product and not just a PA tape.

MY BROTHER CHUCKY

Late one night at about 1:30 in the morning, I received a call from my parents telling me that it was an emergency and asking me to come over. Not having a clue of what type of emergency it was, I quickly got dressed and headed on over to their house. One thing that I have always been apprehensive about is receiving phone calls in the very late night hour or early morning hours. Usually when you receive a call like that it means something serious has happened. That's the first thought that always enters my mind when the phone rings during those hours.

I immediately drove over to my parents' house and noticed that not only were my parents up wide awake, but my Aunt Doris and Uncle Eugene were also there. My father was just sitting at the dining table not saying anything, and my mom was sitting in the living room talking with my aunt. I immediately asked my mom what was going on, but no one really answered me.

I then asked my mom where my sister was. She said that she had just gotten off the phone with my sister and my sister went into shock. Without asking any other questions, I immediately rushed out of the house and jumped in my car to drive to my sister's house. As I was heading out the neighborhood, I spotted my brother Kenny walking up the street, so I pulled over to ask him exactly what was going on. I told him that it looked like Dad had been crying and that Mom said that our sister was in shock. That's when he broke down to me exactly what was going on.

"Chucky was in a car accident tonight," he stated. "And he didn't make it."

Thrown off by what he said to me, I immediately pulled off and continued towards my sister's house. By the time I reached there, the first thing that I noticed was she didn't appear to be in shock like my mother told me. As a matter of fact, she appeared just as calm and controlled of herself as she normally did. She simply stated that she wanted to go to the hospital to see Chucky, so she and I rode there together.

By the time we got to the hospital, my father, brother, and uncle were already there in a closed off room viewing his body, and my sister and I went inside. That's when it finally hit me. Seeing his body lay motionless on the table meant it was true. My brother Chucky was gone.

Earlier that night, Chucky and three of his friends were speeding on the B/W Parkway, which is a two-lane highway that connects Baltimore and DC. They were switching lanes back-and-forth passing cars and reached a point where there were two cars ahead of them in both lanes. They were going so fast that in order to avoid crashing into the back of either one of them, they swerved to the side of the road. Since the B/W Parkway has no shoulder lane in certain parts, the car veered at top speed into the woods, crashed into a tree, split in half, and exploded, thus throwing all four of them out of the car. Only one survived. We never found out exactly who was driving, and to me it really didn't matter who. My man was gone. The kid that I had grown up sharing a bunk bed with was gone. Although he was at the studio with Little Benny and The Masters when we recorded the *Take Me Out To The Go-Go* album, he never got the chance to hear the finished product when it finally came out.

I was numb for a long time after that. I didn't know how to feel because I never experienced death so closely before. All I could do about it was sit back and listen over and over to all the music that we created together. His songs were the things that kept me up. The fact that I had those, and being able to listen to them whenever I wanted to, made him immortal.

THE END OF THE MASTERS

Things were slowly but surely starting to wind down for Little Benny and The Masters. There were times when we would have practice and not every member would show up. I noticed Benny starting to grow a little weary of it. All that he had been through in the music business over the past several years of being his own manager, dealing with band members being tardy or not showing up at all, and having to go through the motions of changing band members, among many other things, were basically taking a toll on him.

One of the first signs that I seriously took note of was James Funk had begun coming to our Metro Club gigs just to check us out. This was during the time when he was no longer playing with Rare Essence and was mainly just doing his deejaying gig. Now normally this would not have been such a big thing to me because it wasn't unusual to be performing and see popular people from the Go-Go community at your gigs showing support, but the difference in this was that Benny would call Funk onto the stage, and Funk would take the lead mic for a while leading us through a song or two. This was something during that time, with the exception of DC's wedding and Rare Essence's Reunion in 1990, that never happened before — not since the days when they both played together with Rare Essence had they been on the same stage together.

Eugene, Damon, Shawn, Raynaldo, Tony, Kato in front - 1977
(photo courtesy of Eugene Randall)

The Stratocasters - 1976
(photo courtesy of Dwayne Lee)

At the Howard Theatre - 1982
Marlo, Kato and Baby John

Little Benny and The Masters - 1988
Kato, Shorty Dud, Benny, Elmo, Vincent
(photo courtesy of Vincent Tabbs)

The Poster Masters, TSE 2014

Little Benny and The Masters live at Laffyette Park, DC - 1991
Benny, Kato, and Michael Muse
(photo courtesy of Michael Muse)

Kato The InnerCity Groover - 1991

Proper Utensils - 1993
Bojack, Al, Jaucques, Jock, Lenny, Scott, Roy Battle, Keith Holmes
Kato, Mike Hughes, Jimmy Jam, Little Benny, Bryan Mills
DJ Gary L Drew, Michael Muse, Jas. Funk, Kojack

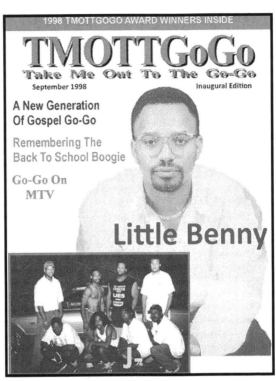

Very first issue of TMOTTGoGo Magazine - 1998

Preston Blue, Weaze, Kato, Mark Ward

Promotional image for WTGO - the very first only Go-Go Radio Program

Kato and Agent 99 - BET Soundstage 2002

Some of the crew members of the TMOTT Morning Show
Preston, Maiah, Kato, Mark, Nena

Chuck Brown at my home with my daughters and their friends
Arica, Tamasha (daughter), Dominique (daughter), Asia

Posing with my daughters and grandson
Krystina, Isaiah, Cherrell, Tamasha
Kato, Dominique

Kato today!

Kato presenting Backyard with *The Band of the Year Award*
at the very first WKYS Go-Go Awards ceremony – 2007

1993-
1995

IN COMES PROPER UTENSILS

One day when hitting The Woodshed for another evening of band practice, I walked into the basement and noticed that James Funk was there. He wasn't saying anything, he was just sitting quietly throughout our entire practice. As we were playing, I got the impression that we were actually auditioning for him since he had been coming to our recent shows. It was being rumored within the band that since he was no longer with Rare Essence, he was probably going to join our band. Or maybe it was just a wish by the band members. We were assuming that maybe he and Benny had been talking about it. Either way, he being in our practice session meant that no doubt something was going on. Outside of Chuck Brown, who is naturally left out of comparisons because he is the ultimate figure in Go-Go, there was no other person at the time who had more juice on the scene than Funk.

With that being the thought process in everyone's mind, our practice session was an all-out concert. We naturally took our playing to the highest level possible. The whole time we played, Funk watched us, and we stared right back at him trying to interpret the expressions he was making regarding our performance.

After practice was over, Funk finally did sit and talk. He mentioned that he and Benny had been discussing the possibility of him joining the band, but the truth of the matter was he was not too impressed with the group enough to want to join.

As a result of him and Benny talking, and unbeknownst to the rest of us, Funk was actually putting a band together of his own. Instead of Funk joining Little Benny and The Masters, Funk wanted Benny to come and join his group.

I was privy to this information, but I kept it to myself because the band that he was putting together was also practicing at The

Woodshed. And since I was the one who was running sound along with Keith at The Woodshed, I was there to witness the building process in its entirety. In fact, no one else outside of those band members had any knowledge whatsoever about the project.

The band was called Proper Utensils. This project was the result of a merge that mainly consisted of former members from already established bands: Rare Essence, Little Benny and The Masters, AM/FM, and Hot Cold Sweat. And although this was the second coming of James Funk's Proper Utensils band (The originally Proper Utensils was around 1981 or 1982), the members were all different this go 'round. They consisted of James Funk, Little Benny, Mike Hughes, Michael Muse, Roy Battle, Bryan Mills, Jock Vaughn, Jimmy Jam, Bojack Butler, and Scott. Each member brought his band's unique flavor into one collective sound, and for the next few months they secretly practiced extensively with no immediate plans of playing anywhere. They simply practiced and tightened up as a unit.

Each and every time the band would practice, I would just be there running the board and taking in everything that I was seeing as a learning experience. The fact of the matter was that I had never seen Funk working in action other than performing on the stage with Rare Essence. Watching him actually put me in awe as to how he ran his camp. It was with no holds barred. He intensely focused on every note, every tempo, and every second of timing of the band. His ear was one with the sound.

During one of the rehearsals, it had gotten to a point where the guitar player was not in agreement with Funk, and he eventually left the band. Someone said, "Now we need to find a new guitar player." Funk replied, "We already have one," and he was looking at me when he said it.

Funk then asked me if I was interested in auditioning for the lead guitar spot in the band. Of course, I was interested. This was one of those situations where you can say I just happened to have been in the right place at the right moment. I was given the instructions to work on a song called "Games" by Chuckii Booker. Not only was I going to have to play it on the guitar, but I was going to have to sing it as well. For the next couple of days, that's what I did. I practiced on that song up and down. I learned the lyrics, and since I was very aware of how Funk likes to have members with the ability to play solos on their instrument, I also created and practiced a guitar solo for the song.

The end of the following practice was when it was my time to get up and audition. As the band accompanied me, I got on the microphone and sang the song while playing my guitar. I immediately felt a strong support from both Benny and Mike Muse as they also got up performing and singing background with me. In fact, by the time we were finished, I really had the impression that I made the band.

Unfortunately, that wasn't the case at all. As I walked into the next practice with my guitar ready to plug up and work, I noticed another guitar player in the room named Jacques Johnson was there to audition. By the time he finished playing, there was no doubt in my mind that the position would not be mine. Jacques was no doubt one of the baddest guitar players that I had ever come across. Watching him play damn near made me want to give up playing my guitar altogether because he was just that wicked on his.

However, even though I did not get the guitar spot in the band, and rightfully so, Funk asked me if I wanted to remain in the band as a rapper based on my performances that he saw with me rapping with

Little Benny and The Masters. It was never said to me by anyone, but I strongly believe that Benny was behind the decision of Funk allowing me to be in the band. So in essence, I became a member of Proper Utensils after all.

Later I found out that what really happened was Mike Hughes did not want me in the band. From what I was told, Mike's feelings was that there would be too many members from Benny's camp in that band, so when he got the word that I was being considered for the guitar spot, he brought Jacques into the camp. Whether that was true or not, I didn't dwell on it or take it personal. Business is business. And without a doubt the one thing you want is a tight band with the tightest musicians that you can gather together. At least that's what I wanted to believe. I really didn't care at all. I was just happy to be in the band.

Jacques coming into the band did not stifle anything. The two of us became such close friends that we lived together at one point. Jacques himself was from a musical family. His father, Jacques Johnson, Sr., was a well-known Jazz sax player. He also was a music instructor at UDC. And Jacques' sister, Michelle Johnson, who also played with Little Benny and The Masters a few years before I started, was also a well-known bass player on the circuit. In fact, she eventually changed her name to Me'shell Ndegéocello and really blew up in the music industry internationally. With all of that, being around Jacques taught me more about my own guitar playing. It is always good to be inspired by other musicians in your circle. You can only get better by doing so.

Knowing the true essence of what it means for a band to be in a tight pocket was something that I learned from Funk. Of course, I knew what a pocket was — a part of a song or performance where a band remains steady with no accents, breakdowns, nor drum rolls. The music is simply neutral, and all members are driving in the same direction. In Go-Go, it is something that is most identified with percussion breaks, and it was during my time with Proper Utensils that I was able to visually understand exactly what it means because Funk gave a visual illustration of it. He'd say, "It's just like when a man and woman are making love. And with all the movement and changing of positions during this lovemaking process, they finally reach a point where the feeling is perfect for the both of them. The feeling is right on point, and they don't want to do anything to change that particular feeling that they're feeling at that moment. There it is! No more changes. No more switching of positions. Just keeping it right there in that position that they are in." Ahhhhh. That's what a tight pocket feels like!

After several months of practicing, Funk decided the band was ready and booked a gig for us to play at the Down Under Club, located in North West, DC. And because of one particular song that was performed at this show, something really magical happened that immediately propelled Proper Utensils into the forefront on the Go-Go scene. The song is "Rumpshaker" by the rap group Wreckx-N-Effect, which was produced by Teddy Riley, and it also contained his rap vocals along with the group.

A live taping of this show was recorded and then given to DJ Gary L Drew, who at the time also worked as a mix deejay for the local radio station 93.9 WKYS. On the night of New Year's Eve, Drew slipped in a tiny piece of this recording during his power mix hour. The section of the recording that was playing when Drew slipped it in? "Rumpshaker."

One week later during band practice session, Drew came into our rehearsal and sat down to talk with us. He first informed us what he had done on New Year's Eve, and then he ran down exactly what followed. Immediately after the tiny section of our band's live recording aired over the radio waves, WKYS began receiving a heavier-than-usual amount of phone calls to the station. As Drew explained it, when a radio station is receiving heavy calling like that, it means one of two things: either another station is running a contest and people are calling the wrong station or people are so excited about the song that they want to hear it again and again. Luckily for us, it was the latter.

Drew went on to explain that although based on that revelation the station immediately added that section of the recording into their rotation playlist, there was a still a dilemma. When a radio station adds a song into rotation, the song has to either already be available for consumers to purchase in record stores, or it has to be released in record stores soon. If neither turn out to be the case, the station pulls the song from its rotation playlist.

This favorably forced Funk's hand to go ahead and take the band into the studio and cut a tighter, much crisper, version. I'm not sure if Funk and Benny didn't want to sample Teddy Riley's voice and MC Lyte's voice, if they wanted to but didn't want to pay more money for the right to do so, or if Teddy Riley and MC Lyte didn't approve. Whatever the case, Benny's rendition of Teddy Riley's "Nah, nah, nah, nah, nah, nah, nah" was looped throughout the song. And a member of Proper Utensils was dating a member of the all-female Go-Go group Pleasure, and he got her to do MC Lyte's "You can start shaking and moving all around."

When people heard it for the very first time, a lot of them originally thought that it was Little Benny and The Masters because of Benny's strong presence throughout the song. No one knew at that time that the band was no longer together, but hearing Funk's voice on the song also made people very curious. And although the song was not an original, the stamp and vamp that we put on the song made it Proper Utensils'. The song was so big that it propelled Proper Utensils to the top of the ranks with the other big bands. "Go-Go Rumpshaker" made us so hot that we were packing houses to capacity, and that was unheard of for a new group. The ladies went crazy when we played it, but then again, they went crazy whenever we played anything. We were putting on good shows with good music, and Funk's rapping had the ladies going wild.

During this time, I met a dude by the name of Mark Ward. He had the same passion for Go-Go music that I did, so we clicked instantly. Not only was he a fan of Go-Go music and culture, he was also a student of both. His knowledge was far more extensive than the average fan. We engaged in deep conversations regarding the way bands executed their music, as well as the different styles of the different bands of different eras. Since he was an avid Motown fan, our discussions always focused on stage presentation and front-line-vocal deliveries. Those deep discussions lasted the entire ride to my Proper Utensil shows, and I would get him into our shows just like my cousin Byron got me into Rare Essence shows. Afterwards we'd talk non-stop about our performance and Go-Go topics until he dropped me off. Mark also became a regular at The Woodshed. He would help out here and there and also work on the sound.

As for Little Benny and The Masters, nothing happened. There was no official break up, Benny just stopped holding rehearsals and booking shows. Just like that, there was no more Little Benny and The Masters. Benny was already tired because of people not coming to rehearsals and issues like that. Now whether he contacted the other guys and just said that he wasn't doing it anymore, I don't know. It was as simple as one day I'm rehearsing with Little Benny and The Masters at The Woodshed, and then a week later I'm at The Woodshed with Proper Utensils, just like that.

FROM PROP TO FAMILY

For the next year, I would take the stage with Proper Utensils delivering rapping cover songs such as the Das Efx's "Mic Check" joint, Naughty By Nature's "Hip-Hop Hurray," ONYX's "Slam," and other songs that Funk would request of me. I would also join in on singing background when Mike Muse would sing slow cover songs such as Mint Condition's "Pretty Brown Eyes."

One of the main things that Funk wanted to focus on with this band was doing strictly all cover songs, and to him it didn't matter whose cover we were doing. In other words, we would do covers of other Go-Go bands as much as covering national artists. His motto was, "If it's a hit, then we're playing it." Since there were many in the band from other bands, we played those songs as well: Rare Essence songs, Little Benny and The Masters songs, Hot Cold Sweat songs, Pleasure songs, it didn't matter.

This also came during a time when many of the younger bands were beginning to make a lot of noise in the city. Bands such as Junkyard, Northeast Groovers, and Backyard Band were gaining more traction for the younger generation of Go-Go fans. The difference with these younger bands was that since they were young themselves, they catered mostly to the young generation. This meant that the majority of their crowd were younger than the majority of ours. Our crowd, which was an older crowd, did not go to see those bands play, but they did like some of the songs they were recording and releasing. Funk's thing was to play some of those songs as well for our older crowd.

This would sometimes feel kind of odd to us because although it was normal to play covers of national artists, it was not normal for one Go-Go band to play the music of another. And sometimes it would feel kind of embarrassing and uncomfortable doing so.

For example, one night when we were playing at Rhythms Nightclub, one of the songs that we were set to play and I was set to rap, was a song by Northeast Groovers called "Van Damn." This song was very hot in the city, and since it was hot, Funk was going to play it. However, standing up on stage rapping the lyrics to the song while seeing members of Northeast Groovers in the crowd getting a real big kick out of it was not setting well with me. They were in the crowd high fiving each other, and I was on the stage feeling like Boo Boo the Fool. I guess to them, they probably took it as we were biting them, but on the contrary, we were actually paying tribute to them to our crowd. Another song by a younger band whose material we played was Junkyard's "Rough It Off." I had to rap that one as well. Eventually without Funk noticing, at least I don't think he noticed, I started taking out their lyrics and replacing them with my own original lyrics.

Our set was different when we played on the road. There was another time when we had a show at Delaware State and we were on the card with Run DMC. As we were on the stage about to go into the Onyx song "Slam," I looked to the side of the stage and noticed Jam Master Jay standing there watching us. This was significant because Jam Master Jay was the person who produced Onyx, and Little Benny and I were about to rap the lyrics of the song. The difference with playing at Delaware State and playing at home was that when we finished our set, Jam Master Jay, who was quiet and laid back around us, actually came up to me and gave me props for the rendition of the Onyx song that we played. He extended his hand and said, "Man, that was nice! Damn!"

In addition to Rhythms Nightclub, the other clubs we played regularly around the city were the Metro Club, the Eastside, and on Sunday nights the Ibex. At the same time, because of the "Go-Go Rumpshaker" release, we were also getting a lot of invitations to play out of town. One of the spots was a club in Richmond, Virginia called *Club Ivories*. This happened to be a really popular spot in

Richmond, and it was the same place DJ Kool later recorded his national hit "Let Me Clear My Throat." They actually wanted us to play out there every week, but the drive to Richmond every week would have proven to be a little bit too demanding.

We also played out of town on cards with Pete Rock & CL Smooth, Chris Tucker, Christopher Williams, Adele Givens, A Tribe Called Quest, De La Soul, Scarface, and Yo-Yo. These trips actually gave us opportunities to network with these national artists, and sometimes I would pass my own personal demo tapes to them.

The fact that Jacques and I had become pretty tight led to other things. We would do a lot of recording in his father's studio. Jacques would lay down all the music tracks, and I would write and lay down all the lyrics. The plan was to have them recorded and then presented to the band with hopes Funk would like them enough to record in the studio.

For example, one of the songs that we played with Proper Utensils was a Snoop Dogg joint. Snatching the tagline of "Bow-wow-wow-yippy-yo-yippy-yay," which was originally a tagline belonging to George Clinton's "Atomic Dog," Jacques created an entire new song around it, and I wrote the lyrics. Other songs that we recorded would be some of my own stuff that he wanted to lay music to.

Eventually, Jacques decided he wanted to hook me up with this girl he knew. He had a girlfriend who lived in Virginia, and thought it would be a good idea to try and hook me up with a friend of hers. With his matchmaking hat on, he set up a date where we would go out there on Thanksgiving so I could meet her.

Not only did I hook up with the girl, but outside of band practice and shows, I found myself taking trips to Virginia every free moment that I had to spend time with her. It had even gotten to the point that I was spending more time there than I was in my own apartment. Before long, the girl told me that she was pregnant. After the different failed relationships that I had, I wanted to make sure that I spent more attention to her than I had done in any of my relationships in the past. This woman was cool, and I was really digging her. I was cool with her so much that I decided I was going to do what I felt I was supposed to do. I cut off my long braids, wrote a resignation letter to Funk stating that I was leaving the band, and I moved to Virginia just that quick.

By this time, I was about 28-years old. Out of all the things that I had done so far, the music thing, the theatre thing, the playwriting thing, and the Go-Go thing, none had taken me to where I hoped to be by this age. So with us about to have a child together, I saw it as my cue from God that it was time for me to go a different route, which I called the regular, normal, family life route. In reality, that family thing was always something I wanted to have anyway. At one point I actually joined the Army in order to achieve it. The purpose for that was to be able to support a family. Besides, that starving artist thing was starting to get old and wear on me.

So there I was still writing my music and still playing my guitar. Our daughter Tamasha was born in December of 1994. That made two children for me, and four for her, but my mission was to take them all in as one and to grow this new family to where I felt God wanted me to. My life was about to significantly take on a whole new direction that I would have never anticipated if I tried.

MOVING ON

Now that I was no longer in the game and relocated to a new area, the first thing I had to do was find a job. The first job I landed was as a preschool teacher. This position lasted only one year. I loved the kids, but I was not particularly too fond of some of their parents. They gave me hell, and part of me knew most of the time it had to do with the fact that I was black. I learned fast that working around other people's children was something that I definitely was not going to enjoy.

After a while of going to work every day and then coming home in the evenings, I found myself wanting so badly to be in a creative environment. I began occupying my spare time writing short stories, and it wasn't too long before I really started missing playing music. Before I knew it, I found myself contacting Funk again to see if I would be able to get back into the band.

Right around this time was when a tragic incident had taken place regarding a prominent figure in the Go-Go community. I received a call from one of Benny's sisters and she told me that Footz, the drummer for Rare Essence, had been killed. This was a tragic incident that shocked and stunned the entire Go-Go community. Everyone was devastated by the news. Though there was not a doubt in my mind of the hurt and pain that everyone was feeling, there was none that could have been more hurt than Funk himself. You see, Footz was Funk's little brother, and in a sense I could understand what he most likely was going through because I basically went through the same thing a couple years prior. With that being such a dark cloud hovering, my trying to bother Funk with something so trivial as my wanting to get back into the band was the last thing on my mind. I decided to leave it alone.

After several failed attempts at trying to obtain new employment, I was finally blessed to be offered and land a job at a company called the Newspaper Association of America. I say blessed because not only was it a blessing to be able to receive another job, but the work I did there turned out to be an awakening for me that actually helped lift my spirits. The moment I started working there, I immediately realized the amount of creativity that I had now found myself surrounded by.

The Newspaper Association of America (aka NAA) was a nonprofit organization that represented nearly 2,000 newspapers across the country. Its main mission was serving as a catalyst for the newspaper industry by identifying industry innovations and providing tools and forums for the exchange of information and ideas.

I started working there in the mailroom, and from the moment I hit the place I immediately found myself engulfed in constant encouragement that the company provided. It was such a creative atmosphere to be in. For example, they published a monthly company newsletter, and I was encouraged to write articles that they would publish in the newsletter. During holidays such as Christmas, they encouraged all the different departments, including us in the mailroom, to enter company contests for the best office decorations, and we would win. While doing my daily deliveries of the mail, I would observe the different departments in the company, and the communications department where they created and published a magazine called *Presstime* piqued my interest the most. I found myself spending a lot of time in that area just to learn and see how the whole process worked.

After only a few months of working there, I found out that the communications department had a job opening available. The position was for Database Operator. Seeing that as an opportunity for me to work closer within the communications department, I applied for the position and I got the job. The job duties of this position consisted of, but were not limited to, supporting the communications department by assisting in the writing, editing, and producing of media content. It also entailed me keeping and updating a tight-structured database system that consisted of all the journalists across the country who were members of the association.

The more I worked there, the more I was able to see how things worked. The more I was able to see how things worked, the more I learned. Although I was just in the position of database operator, my ultimate goal was to eventually get into a position to be either one of the writers of the magazine, or one of the layout designers. I would spend a bunch of time just watching and seeing how they would put stories together, the way they would lay them out in magazine format, and how they completed a full, glossy, printed magazine. That intrigued me to no end.

Also located inside of the same building was another company just like ours called the NABJ (National Association of Black Journalists). This was actually funny to me because on one side of the building was NAA, a majority white aspect of journalism, and the other side of the building was NABJ, a majority black aspect of journalism. Finding out about them, my attention shifted a little.

I badly wanted to work for the NABJ because in discovering the company, I thought that was exactly where I was supposed to be. I saw it as my avenue to be able to network and function with all the different black journalists across the county, and I honestly felt that the reason God had me at NAA was so that I could work my way into the NABJ so I could eventually become one of them.

I was so passionate and engulfed in wanting to work for and be part of the NABJ that I would hang around their end of the building on my free time hoping that they would eventually give me some type of opportunity to work for them. Whenever they had any job openings, I would always be one of the first to apply. Unfortunately, that never happened. I actually felt kind of shunned by them, but I still took it in stride. I always figured if I can't get in one way, I'll figure out another. What I did learn from that experience though was the understanding of the passion a person could have in wanting to be a part of something. That was a feeling that to this day I had never forgotten.

1996 & BEYOND

THE BIRTH OF TMOTTGOGO

One of the main things that eventually proved to be a major asset for me working in the communications department was that I was now in a position where I was learning new technology when it came to doing my job on the computer. The biggest plus of them all was when I discovered a new system that NAA was using called the Internet. This was a system that the company was using directly for the purpose of maintaining constant contact with the members of the association who were located across the country. They had what was called a website, and another part of my job detailed implementing the database information into this website. This provided the opportunity for association members to visit using a computer from anywhere in the world and be able to pull up detailed updates of NAA information regarding registrations, upcoming workshops and conventions, the latest journalistic reports, as well as information where they could directly be in communication with the individual departments within the NAA.

I had been working at different jobs operating on computers for a few years, mainly with word processing and spreadsheet platforms, but this was different. It wasn't the usual black and white DOS screen that I had been used to. It was a colorful screen full of images and sound clips that gave the feel of being inside of a magazine or a virtual catalog. I could open up a browser, which was called Netscape, type in any subject, and a list of websites would appear on the screen detailing information on the subject I entered. It was the most phenomenal thing I'd ever seen in my life.

Just for fun, sometimes I would type in any subject that popped in my head, curious to see what would appear on the computer screen. If I typed television programs, what came up was a list of websites that were about television shows. If I typed automobiles, what came up was a list of websites containing information about cars and trucks. It felt like I was leaving the office and actually going to these places without ever really getting out of my chair. I had gotten so excited about it that I couldn't wait to type the words "Go-Go Music" just to see what type of information would come up, but when I did, nothing came up. I didn't think much of it at the time. I just continued searching for other things on the Internet.

Another thing, which became a very significant occurrence, is that the NAA gave me the option of having my own brand new personal computer at home. They had a program where they would buy you a computer and simply deduct the payments from your paycheck over 12 months with no interest. Since I never had a computer, that was an opportunity I would've been dumb as a mug to pass up, so I took advantage of it without hesitation.

Working so much in updating information on the company's website, I started growing a really strong interest in learning how to build my own website. The problem was that with my new computer at home, I had no way of even knowing what I needed to do to even pull up the Netscape browser. Not only that, I also had no idea or way of knowing whatsoever how to even start creating my own website. I just knew that apparently it could be done because the NAA had a website as well as so many other companies.

Since I had no clue as to how or what was needed to build a website, I basically blew it off. I was more intrigued with finding out all the different things that I could pull up. While at work I discovered a software called America Online (AOL) that could be installed on your computer, and if connected to what was called a modem from your computer to your telephone line, it would dial up and connect to a browser of its own. It wasn't the Netscape browser, but it still gave you the opportunity to search and pull up websites.

Another thing about having AOL was that not only did it allow you to be able to search and pull up websites, it actually had a whole world of its own. You could play video games such as solitaire and Frogger. There was a whole bunch of other people in this AOL world, and they would be in this area called a chat room having conversations with each other simply by typing in their words. What really caught my eye about the AOL world was that it had an area where you could have your own webpage. Bingo! I felt that I hit the jackpot. My next mission was to sign up to have my own webpage built through AOL. The only problem was that I had to figure out exactly what my webpage would be and talk about, but I figured that out in about 5 seconds. In truth, it wasn't a problem at all because the only thing I knew about was exactly what I had been doing pretty much all of my life — I decided that my webpage was going to be about Go-Go music.

In determining a name for the webpage, I decided to base it on one of my favorite songs by Rare Essence. I titled it "Kato's Take Me Out To The Go-Go." I then designed an intro page where I placed a picture of Little Benny on the front with the words under him reading *Where you wanna go? Where you wanna go?* Anyone who was familiar with Rare Essence would automatically know that at the top of this particular song, Benny yells those words to the crowd, and the crowd yells back, "Take me out to the go-go!"

Under those words I placed a button to symbolize giving the answer to the question that was being asked. Once a person clicked on that button it would open up the main webpage, hence taking them to the go-go.

On the webpage itself, I simply wrote a definition describing what Go-Go music was, and added several pictures of different bands, including, of course, Little Benny and The Masters and Proper Utensils. That was basically it, and as far as I was concerned the Internet now included a website on the subject of Go-Go. The only things I would do from there was add new pictures and music clips here and there.

As time went on, I would visit other music sites to get ideas of what would be cool to also have on my site. That was when I stumbled across the site called DCMusicWeb.com. On this particular site, there would be a bunch of article reviews that people had written. They would go out to different live events across the DC, Maryland, and Virginia area and write reviews on them. The website had a writer for almost every category from Rock, Folk, Bluegrass, Jazz, and Country, but there were no write-ups anywhere on the site that reviewed Go-Go events. I contacted the owner of that site via email and submitted my interest of also becoming a writer of the site. I proposed to him that I would go out to the different go-gos across the city and submit article reviews that he could then place on this site.

After an agreement was made, I would drive into the city, connect with my buddies Weaze and Mark Ward, and we would hit some of the Go-Go spots. Weaze and Mark would take pictures, and I would take notes. Then I would drive home later that night, write the articles, and submit them to DC Music Web.

My first review was written on a Proper Utensils show that we attended. I figured that would be an easy place to start since I was formerly a member of the band. Since the internet was so new and there were no Go-Go websites, one could say that this was the very first online Go-Go review.

The next article I decided to write about was a brand new group that was making noise in the city at the time called Maiesha & The Hip Huggers. The special thing about them, besides the fact that they consisted of members from EU, including Sugar Bear, JuJu, and Junie, was that they had a gimmick where they dressed in 70s style attire and played 70s covers in the Go-Go format. Again, Weaze, Mark, and I hit the spot. They took pictures, and I took notes. Like before, later that night I wrote the article and submitted it to DC Music Web.

After about my third article review submission, something suddenly occurred to me. Why was I writing articles and submitting them to another website when I could just write them and place them on my own website? From that point on when Weaze, Mark, and I would hit different Go-Go spots, I would write articles and place them on the *Kato's Take Me Out To The Go-Go* website.

TMOTTGOGO

After a while I started getting the feeling that even though I was placing articles on the website, it was not getting the kind of attention I was hoping to obtain. By this time I realized that although I was putting articles on the site for others to come and read, one of the things that I was lacking was stability on the main internet surface outside of AOL. I discovered that I was actually being stifled because of where my webpage was located. In other words, although it was still accessible on the internet, it was harder to find because it was under AOL and not a separate entity of its own. The only way that folks could know about it was if they were being told about. It was not able to be pulled by searching for it through Netscape.

Through the learnings at my job, I found out about separate hosting of websites as well as domain names, where the website could actually stand out on its own. There was a company called Network Solutions that provided website and domain name hosting. I realized that I needed to obtain a domain name that had to be *something.com*. I also knew that trying to call the site *"Kato's" Take Me Out To The Go-Go.com* was going to be a bit too much. It would be too long of a name to try and get people to type and pull up, so what I ended up doing was dropping "Kato" from the title. To make the name even shorter, I took the first letters off of each word *T-M-O-T-T*, and kept the word *Go-Go* in there. Then I registered it as my domain name, officially creating TMOTTGoGo.com.

Slowly but surely, the more we hit the Go-Go spots and placed the articles on the website, the more word started circulating in the Go-Go community about the website. In the process of writing reviews, we also began doing direct interviews with the bands and artists.

Before long, not only was I writing articles for the website, but others started contacting me to submit articles just as I had done with the DCMusicWeb.com website. One of the first people to contact me about writing an article was a young lady name Chante Cunningham (Smith). She was a member of a group of girlfriends that called themselves The All-Around Honies. They were one of the many different groups of people that you could find at a Go-Go event, and since that was the case, there was no doubt in my mind that her knowledge and experience of the Go-Go scene would add even more flavor to TMOTTGoGo.

Another person who contacted me was actually a friend of Mark's. Her name was Lakishia Fogg, and just like Chante, Lakishia's knowledge of the Go-Go culture was rich and deep. Another great thing about Lakishia was her strong sense of organization, which actually kept me in check regarding the website as a whole. She stayed on me about keeping up the website. She had a strong passion and belief in not only the website but me as a leader as well.

The third person to contact me regarding submitting articles for the site was a guy named David Smith. In his articles, he would do reviews of current Go-Go releases such as Chuck Brown's "Huh Man," Backyard Band's "Hood Related," and Tony Blunt's "Give 'Em What They Want." Other writers who would later join in to submit articles as well were Bobbie Westmoreland, Nena Brown, and Jennifer Angellatta-Moore.

The only thing that bothered me about all of this was the fact that I was not able to pay people monetarily for the articles they submitted. Although TMOTTGoGo did pay monthly costs for the ability to stay active online, it was not receiving income. Therefore, the only thing that I could offer people was the ability to use the TMOTTGoGo platform as a steppingstone to create any type of brand or direction they wanted to take for themselves. Another benefit of them writing articles and reviews was the fact that since TMOTTTGoGo had begun developing a known name in the Go-Go community, I was able to sometimes set up situations where they could attend functions for free depending on who the band was and the trust and relationship that we were growing with them.

One day I received a call from a woman named Felicia Mohammed. She and her husband got on the phone and began talking to me about the TMOTTGoGo website. The words they said to me that day stuck with me because at that time I had no clue what they were talking about. They told me, "You have no idea how important what you're doing really is, young brother. But whatever you do, please don't stop doing it."

That comment stuck with me ever since mainly because they were right. I had no idea of how important what I was doing really was. Heck, I had no idea who they even were, but based on the direction they had given me, something in me told me that I better follow it and keep doing what I was doing. I figured that I'd eventually figure out what they meant later.

It had gotten to the point where I was consumed with learning everything that I could to make TMOTTGoGo the best possible attraction that I could. Before I realized it, I found myself doing exactly the same thing I had done in the past. There I was with another woman, this time married with a family, and I was consuming myself in yet a new goal, but I couldn't help myself. The more I worked on the website, the more I wanted to work on the website. If I wasn't at work, I was either out covering Go-Go artists and events, or in the basement working on the website. Eventually, like the others, she got tired of my antics. After having a second daughter Dominique together, we ultimately went our separate ways.

Everything I saw that could be done on the internet, I wanted to learn how to do, so I would teach myself how to do it and then implement it on TMOTTGoGo. When it came to my site, I believed in what I called the Trojan horse effect, which means the object of the game was to always find ways to attract people to the site.

Once I had them on the site, I had their undivided attention to show them all of the great things that were available ranging from trivia questions, video games, polls, and, of course, Go-Go music. Actually what turned out to be the biggest attraction that brought people in droves to TMOTTGoGo was the message board. The message board peaked at what I call the pre-social media era of the internet. This was a place where people could come, register their names, and engage in daily conversation with each other. It was the next step up from chat rooms, only better because chat rooms moved too fast, making it difficult for people to follow specific topics, while message boards allowed people to create topics that were stationary and easy to follow. The topics that people talked about would range from the latest songs, the latest fashions, and the most recent Go-Go event, to heated discussions such as whose favorite band was better than whose, etc.

The only problem that came with message boards as far as TMOTTGoGo was concerned, was that because many people in the Go-Go community were still not fully knowledgeable of the internet and how it worked, if a person posted a bad statement about a person or band, I would end up getting blamed for making the statement simply because the website was mine.

Another thing that I implemented on the website was Go-Go awards. I would set up polls on the site allowing people to vote for their favorite Go-Go bands, artists, and songs. Once the votes were tallied, I purchased award plaques for the winners. What was more important than the politics of trying to put together some type of an awards event was the presentation of the award winners itself. And since I couldn't afford to host an all-out award show, I saw this as the next best step — Weaze, Mark, and I would attend the shows of the winners and present them with their awards during their breaks. We would hit the Metro Club to present Northeast Groovers with the awards they won. We would hit the Icebox to present Backyard and

Junkyard with the awards they won. And we would hit other spots such as The Classics, and present individuals such as Sugar Bear, Little Benny, and anyone else that won with their awards.

Eventually doing the website just wasn't enough for me. My working at the NAA snagged me into another area because I figured people that were not on the internet needed to have all of this Go-Go information at their fingertips. Consequently, I needed to develop an actual TMOTTGoGo magazine. Seeing how the constructing and laying out of a magazine process worked at my job, I began to take that information and implement it in what I was doing at home.

Wanting to do a magazine format of the website really didn't come as a surprise to me because I was always infatuated with magazines. In fact, during the time that I was playing with Proper Utensils, there was a local zine called "Straight from the Street," and every time that I went into a record store, one of the things that I would do was check to see if they had a new issue. I wanted so badly to be a writer for that zine that I contacted the publisher and set up an interview with him. However in the process of that interview, it turned out that instead of me being a writer, he wanted to hire me to sell ads. That was not what I was interested in so I declined.

Since I started the *TMOTTGoGo* website, which actually published the same type of content you'd find in a regular magazine, I was in the position to put out my own magazine. With that thought, I went into motion. Using a few of the articles that I placed on the website, I created a mockup demo magazine for the purpose of being able to try to generate enough interest in people to buy ads once I put out a real copy.

I had a few dozen copies of the demo magazine printed and I took them into the field to solicit ads. While in in the field, I ran across a guy named Richard O'Connor, who was at the time working with a band called Intimate Groove. The moment that I showed Richard the mockup demo, he took a great interest in what he thought could be a good move. He began to school me in not only the process of trying to solicit ads, but also where to circulate and how to circulate the inaugural issue of the magazine once it got printed.

Setting up the articles for the inaugural issue of the magazine turned out to fall into place as well. The first person that I wanted to have on the cover of the very first issue was Little Benny. After contacting and setting up an appointment with him, Mark and I went to his house and conducted the interview in his dining room.

Another article that I decided to also have placed in this inaugural issue was a piece that was written by a young lady named Tahira Mahdi. I met Tahira through her brother Rashid. At the time he was working on a mini-documentary about Go-Go music for a program that MTV was airing. In his process of gathering information, he contacted us through TMOTTGoGo, and we helped connect him with some of the Go-Go bands. Just like Chante and Lakishia, Tahira contacted me while this was going on and stated her interest for writing with TMOTTGoGo. She submitted an article about the difference between the DC culture and the Baltimore culture entitled "It's Only An Hour Away."

The other articles that were selected to be published in the inaugural magazine issue were an interview piece with the J-Mob Band, a story on a gospel Go-Go band called Submission, a story reminiscing about The Back To School Boogie, a spotlight on DJ Rico, a poster-size picture of Dig-Dug (percussionist for Northeast Groovers), and a review of a CD that was just released by Rare Essence called "We Go On And On." On the back cover was a large picture of DC artist Keith-Nine. Along with a few other small pieces, the inaugural issue of the magazine was ready to go to print.

The 36-page inaugural magazine was released in September of 1998. Because I had generated little to no ads at all, I used what money I had and printed 5,000 issues. Banking on the premise that the main object was to get this magazine into as many hands as possible, the plan was to give them away for free. This would allow us to easily have them placed in just about every store magazine rack through the city because the main objective was to get the *TMOTTGoGo* name branded. From there, we would be in a better position toward building in the future. Weaze, Mark, myself, and now Richard, all set out and distributed the magazines to shops and record stores across the city. We placed them in the HOBO clothing shop, the All Daz clothing shop, Sam Goody Music, DDTP clothing shop, Mind Boggler, The Foot Stop, Future Sports, Kemp Mill Records, and any other shop that we could think of. Many of the stores used the TMOTTGoGo Magazine as an incentive to give away to customers who purchased products from those shops.

By the time all was said and done, mission was accomplished. We achieved what we set out to do. We let it be known that TMOTTGoGo, the trusted voice of the Go-Go community, was on the scene.

After the success of the inaugural magazine, Richard introduced me to a guy named Preston Blue. He not only worked directly in the music industry, but he brought into the TMOTTGoGo camp priceless amounts of industry knowledge. Soon we all had become a tightknit group developing plans and ideas, and then implementing them. We took "Nos" and turned them into "Yeses."

As things continually progressed with TMOTTGoGo, I started understanding what Felicia Mohammad and her husband were talking about on that phone call. The object of TMOTTGoGo was becoming clear to me. Even though I started it with only the desire of merely wanting to learn how to build websites, it was becoming more than just a website. There was now an objective for what I and others were doing with it. In essence, TMOTTGoGo had become a gateway to an urban music culture. The object of it was to serve as a window for Go-Go. This means that not only would the vehicle be used for others outside of the culture to look in and see what we were doing, but it would also be used by folks within this music culture to be able to look out and see what's going on.

With that in mind, we took every opportunity technically available to us to explore new avenues and create platforms for the purpose of continuing the visibility of the music genre and its culture so that it got the respect that it deserved.

For example, instead of constantly begging local radio to pay more respect and not just use the music when it was beneficial to them, we took it upon ourselves to counter what they were not offering, and in 1998, we created the first online radio program that catered to strictly Go-Go music.

Titled WTGO Go-Go Radio, Weaze, Mark, Tahira, Preston and I would gather every Friday night at The Woodshed and stay up until 1 or 2 o'clock in the morning formatting and pre-recording our Go-Go radio show and then embed it on the TMOTTGoGo website, making it available for people to tune in days later.

With Go-Go music being our backdrop, we would create skits and characters that would serve as comedic entertainment in between the Go-Go music that we kept in constant rotation.

Because of her ability to be able to snag and obtain interviews with some people who could sometimes be difficult to interview, we considered Tahira our secret weapon. Thus, I gave her the name "Agent 99."

For example, one time while conducting an interview session with boxer Mark "Too Sharp" Johnson, Tahira accompanied me. This particular interview turned out to be a difficult one because Too Sharp was in the middle of training for an upcoming fight and had very little to say in regards to the questions I was asking. He had very short answers, and some people just aren't interview friendly. What happened at that point was Tahira decided to take over and do the interview. As soon as she turned her tape recorder on and started asking questions, he basically turned into Stephen A. Smith of ESPN. That was when we realized that because of Tahira's sharp intelligence, beauty, charm, and sex appeal, she could get interviews from folks, especially men, that would normally be difficult for us to accomplish. She was our secret weapon. She still is Agent 99.

In order to bring more flavor and diversity into our Go-Go radio format, I changed the name from *WTGO* to *Kato and The TMOTT Crew Morning Show*, and brought in an even larger cast: Nena Brown, Tara Thompson (Berger), Maiah Coles, Terrance Berger, and DaMont Wood, who served as an on-location correspondent for the show. We did in-person interviews with artists such as Donnell Floyd, Scooby, Y'anna Crawley, and James Funk.

Chuck Brown believed in TMOTTGoGo and really threw his support behind it from day one. In fact, he even went out of his way and came to my house for an interview. The cast of the Kato and the TMOTT Morning Crew show took great care of him. Believe me when I say having a conversation with Chuck Brown in my living room was an outstanding experience. It was so important that not only did all of the personalities of the show attend the interview, but some of our little kids were able to meet and listen to Chuck. Nothing in the world beats having my two grade-school daughters in awe of Chuck's presence and his stories. Absolutely nothing!

FATAL ATTRACTION

In addition to doing the radio shows, we got ourselves involved with working with young, upcoming bands. One of the main ones was a group of young guys and a girl from Crossland High School who called themselves Fatal Attraction. Originally working and recording under Preston and Richard's label called Bag Of Beats Records, Preston, Mark and I took interest in their potential and began working hands on with them.

Working with Fatal Attraction was great because of the fact that they were still in the learning and building stages and had not reached the "I know it all" mentality yet. In being able to work with them, I was able to imply to them some of the things that I learned over the years when it comes to affective, productive, and most importantly, memorable performances at go-gos. Stage presence, choreography, and the delivery of the songs being played were some of the things I learned while observing bands growing up, as well as playing in bands, that many upcoming bands of the younger generations had not taken into consideration. Somewhere along the line, these were some of the things that had gotten lost with the newer generations of bands, so I took what I knew and paid it forward to them.

Fatal Attraction created a song called "Twilight Zone," and in the middle of the song, they transitioned into singing the chorus to the Loose Ends song "Slow Down." While in rehearsal, I envisioned that part of the song as an opportunity for the band to execute a theatre-style presentation in their stage performance — as they sang the lyrics to "Slow Down," every person on stage were to begin moving around in slow motion, and to do so in a very exaggerated manner in order for it to effectively work. The band felt this was a really stupid idea, but they went along with the instructions and executed it at the next live show. To their surprise, it was not only well received from the crowd, but it became expected from them by their fans. From that point on, when Fatal Attraction did their slow motion movements, the crowd would join in and move around in slow motion with them.

TMOTTGOGO HONORS I

In 2006 we marked the 10 year anniversary of TMOTTGoGo, and we commemorated the anniversary in early 2007 by having The TMOTTGoGo Honors at the historical Lincoln Theatre. We used it as a platform to present lifetime achievement awards to four individuals who, under Chuck Brown, led the forefront of this entire Go-Go movement, and whom I deem as the Four Horsemen of Go-Go: Sugar Bear from Experience Unlimited, Tony Fisher from Trouble Funk, James Funk from Rare Essence, and Little Benny originally from Rare Essence.

The four bands that played on the card of that event were Junkyard Band, Da Grewp, The What Band, and Rare Essence. Between each band's set, there was a platform presentation to an honoree, followed by a video montage of that honoree, and then we presented the honoree with a Lifetime Achievement Award in the form of a statue.

No longer was I seeing things as a case of us needing the acceptance of others to feel accomplished about ourselves. If the media wouldn't respect and accept Go-Go, so be it. We'd create our media. If the Grammy's wouldn't accept Go-Go, so be it. We'd create our own award ceremonies. If mainstream radio won't respectfully accept it, so be it. We'll create our radio. And the beauty of it all is we'll not only be just fine, but we'll be able to celebrate Go-Go culture without their say nor their influence.

Throughout my entire life growing up in this music culture, the one thing that I learned was that if you want something done, you're going to have to do it yourself. We have accomplished and achieved many things over the years in spite of countless obstacles.

SALUTE TO LITTLE BENNY & CHUCK BROWN

On the morning of Sunday May 30, 2010, I received a call from Ron Moten of the Peaceoholics that hit me like a ton of bricks. He called to give me the news that Little Benny passed away. If it had not been Ron who called me about it, I would not have believed it. And no matter how much I tried to deny it, it was indeed true.

Benny was bigger than life when it came to Go-Go. I immediately started reminiscing about things such as the very first time I ever saw him perform at Prince George's Community College, the time we first spoke when he asked if I was interested in playing in his band, the many shows we performed together, both with Little Benny and The Masters as well as Proper Utensils, the road trips we took to out-of-town gigs, the way his entire family had always taken me in as if I was a part of the family, and many other memories.

Even after I was no longer playing in bands with him, not only did he agree to do the cover and feature story for the very first TMOTTGoGo Magazine I published, Benny was a cat who supported just about everything that I did. Whenever we would have our TMOTTGoGo functions and cookouts, he would show up in support. Anything that had anything to do with supporting the Go-Go Coalition, he would be available. There were even times when he would ask me if I was still playing my guitar. I would always answer by saying that I needed to tighten up on my chops before even thinking about playing again, and he would respond, "Oh, don't worry about all that. You can rap. All you need to do is scratch on your guitar and just start rapping. That's all you need to do."

Benny's funeral service was held at the Washington Convention Center. Now you have to really be a big person in the city for them to have to hold your funeral services at the Convention Center. That shows you just how big Little Benny was in the city.

I didn't want to sit in the front because I did not want to view the body. When I think about a person, I want my mind to be able to remember the person the way they were the last time I saw them. That's just the picture that I want to be in my head, so I sat toward the back.

As I took my seat, I was handed a program booklet that had been put together for the services, which consisted of a pictorial of his entire life. As I began reading through the booklet and looking at all the pictures, I turned the page and my heart dropped. My eyes started watering. In the booklet was a large picture of the inaugural issue of TMOTTGoGo Magazine that Benny did the cover story for 12 years earlier. That was a program booklet about his life. Seeing that magazine cover in there with all the other pictures depicting his life told me something.

Here is a guy who I was inspired by before I started playing in bands with him, I was inspired while playing in bands with him, and I continued to be inspired by him even after I stopped playing in the bands with him. He really played a major role in my life, but seeing my TMOTTGoGo Magazine in there told me that in some kind of funny, little way, apparently somewhere along the line I played a role in his as well. And knowing that means the world to me.

On the day Chuck Brown passed away, I received a message from my 12-year-old daughter that asked *Daddy, did Chuck Brown pass away?* She was only about 7-years old when she met him at our house. Later that evening, both my younger daughters' social media statuses read — *Rest in peace, Chuck Brown. I'm glad I got the chance to meet you.* Those words instantly touched me because they reminded me of just how many generations Chuck has touched, and that's a big deal. In his first hit song "Bustin Loose," Chuck repeats over and over "Give me the bridge." Well, Chuck Brown was and remains that bridge for all of us in the Go-Go culture, as well as people of all ages and walks of life in the DMV region. I will always be thankful for that for the rest of my life, and I will truly miss him.

TMOTTGOGO HONORS II

In March of 2014, TMOTTGoGo held its second Honors event, this time at the historical Howard Theatre. The individuals within the Go-Go community selected to be honored this time were Michael "Funky Ned" Neal from Rare Essence, William "JuJu" House from Experience Unlimited, Donnell Floyd from Rare Essence, 911, and Familiar Faces, "Sweet" Charie Mitchell-Agurs from Chuck Brown and Be'la Dona, Thomas Sayers Ellis who is a great Photographer and Poet, and Jason "Cocky" Lewis from 3DB.

In addition to the presentation given to the honorees, The 2nd TMOTTGoGo Honors highlighted many of the upcoming bands and gave them the opportunity to perform at The Howard Theatre. The bands that performed were Dynasty Band, Kendall The Jack of All Trades, All4U, and Obsession Band. Others who performed at TMOTTGoGo Honors II are Sugar Bear, Maysa, Killa Cal, Sylver Logan Sharp, Terri S., and Deborah Bond.

Washington in the 80's

I, along with Marion Barry and Joe Gibbs, was selected to be a part of the *Washington In The 80's* is a documentary focused on Washington, DC and the people and events that made the city tick during the decade of the 1980s. Other prominent figures of the DC area that participated include Kojo Nnamdi, Maureen Bunyan, Pat Buchanan, Arch Campbell, Doug Williams, Carol Schwartz, and many others. In the documentary I discussed the significant marks of the Go-Go community.

Unsung *The Story of Chuck Brown*

Unsung, TV One's signature music biography series, is producing an episode on Chuck Brown, and it was an honor for me to participate in the production. The show sheds light on some of the most influential and talented artists ever, and it's going to be nice to see nation-wide attention placed on Chuck and the Go-Go culture.

Two decades has passed, and TMOTTGoGo is still shining light on Go-Go as well as providing a stepping stone to any individual, business, and band in the industry. The TMOTTRadio.com online radio station plays continuous Go-Go music 24/7, and that makes me happier than anyone can imagine. It also allows people to host radio shows of their own where their voices can be heard.

So what am I doing now? Well, I remain active in the Go-Go industry. I served as a chair member of the Go-Go Coalition, I was a board member and adviser to several of the Go-Go Awards ceremonies, and I'm still a liaison for many media sources outside of the Go-Go industry.

I provide services in graphic designing and web designing for many different entrepreneurs, artists, and businesses. I may be the person that designed the flyer for the event you're heading to and the designer of a few websites you've visited. I also create product and marketing strategies for individual groups and artists within the music industry.

Musically, I use the gift God has given me towards His services as the drummer for the choirs of Chantilly Baptist Church. I really find it rewarding, and my experiences growing up in Go-Go have allowed me to be fruitful and effective. I've also began another show with Tahira, aka Agent 99, called *99 and Kato – The Radio Experience*. I often lend my knowledge and expertise to documentaries, articles, and books on social media marketing, entrepreneurism, and, yes, Go-Go music and culture. What's next for Kato? Who knows? Lectures, workshops, seminars, and festivals…I lived and experienced so much that I may even write a book.

Made in the USA
Lexington, KY
26 November 2019